THE LASTING LEGACIES OF MULK RAJ ANAND

A TRIBUTE

THE LASTING LEGACIES OF MULK RAJ ANAND

A TRIBUTE

Edited by

Md. Rizwan Khan

ATLANTIC

PUBLISHERS & DISTRIBUTORS (P) LTD

Published by

ATLANTIC

PUBLISHERS & DISTRIBUTORS (P) LTD

B-2, Vishal Enclave, Opp. Rajouri Garden,
New Delhi-110027
Phones : +91-11-25413460, 25429987, 25466842

Sales Office
7/22, Ansari Road, Darya Ganj,
New Delhi-110002
Phones : +91-11-23273880, 23275880, 23280451
Fax : +91-11-23285873
Web : www.atlanticbooks.com
E-mail : info@atlanticbooks.com

Branch Office
5, Nallathambi Street, Wallajah Road,
Chennai-600002
Phones : +91-44-64611085, 32413319
E-mail : chennai@atlanticbooks.com

ISBN 978-81-269-0983-4

Printed in India
at Nice Printing Press, Delhi

Foreword

This is not a foreword in the conventional sense of the word. Most forewords are, as Mulk told Jasbir Jain, 'crutches, which good scholars should avoid'. In fact, they are no more than a device for selling a book by getting an eminent personality—whether literary, political or social—to recommend it to the reading public. I am by no means such a personality: half of the contributors to this anthology are better known than I am. What I say here is what I feel about this book of essays on a man with whom I had a love-hate relationship for forty years.

While preparing an anthology of short stories for The Bodley Head, its editor, James Mitchie, once told me that an anthology is always a mixed bag, and that if it could boast of even six good stories, its publication would be justified. Using this analogy, the present volume is a very welcome addition to the existing studies on Mulk Raj Anand. Rizwan Khan's Introduction provides us an honest and succinct portrait of this controversial writer, and, along with some perceptive comments on Anand's major novels, it sets the stage for the essays that follow.

The volume opens with a short but moving piece by Shiv K. Kumar entitled 'Fall of a Titan'. Some purists might snigger at Mulk being referred to as a 'Titan', but many of us feel that way, and Shiv in his eulogy has caught our anguish and our irreparable sense of loss. Dolly Sahair's 'Mulk's Day in Khandala' is written with great sensitivity, but cast in an altogether different mould. It makes hurtful reading: the once strong and argumentative voice gone strangely silent, waiting for the world to inexorably close round him. Both these pieces in a sense belong to the present, to death and decay, while Meenakshi Mukherjee's 'Call Me Uncle Mulk' takes us back to the era when Mulk was in full fighting form. And it is this Mulk, with all his contradictions, that is the subject of this anthology.

Meenakshi's portrait of Mulk, showing his immediate spleen and his final generosity, tallies completely with the Mulk I knew. On the publication of my *So Many Freedoms: A Study of the Major Fiction of Mulk Raj Anand* (1977) he came down on me heavily because I had failed to appreciate some of his later works. In his letters to me he has called me a 'Brown Sahib', 'illiterate', 'superficial', 'immature', and excused himself with these words, 'There are some limits to one's humility before perverse critics like you.' In a copy of *Conversations in Bloomsbury* (1981), presented to me fifteen years after its publication, he wrote, 'For the critic who thinks everything I have written is rubbish!'

Nothing could be further from the truth. But truth never got in the way of an angry Mulk, though it always reasserted itself later. And then came the apology and the warm hug. I often fretted over what Mulk said to me, but Dolly Sahair (Mulk's closest friend and confidante) kept reassuring me not to take his comments seriously. But not all his comments were harsh. 'Morgan [Foster] saw me published, and you resurrected me,' he said to me at the time I placed three of his novels with The Bodley Head. This praise of me is as false as his comment that I thought his writing was rubbish. The Bodley Head reprinted *Untouchable*, *Coolie* and *Private Life of an Indian Prince* because they saw each novel as a minor masterpiece. I hope the foregoing diversion will provide some comfort to Meenakshi (whose works I admire) and to others who found themselves in a similar predicament. Mulk believed in the lasting value of friendship as much as Forster did, but he did not possess Forster's poise and calm demeanor. He was impulsive; he was also a man of strong passions.

An understanding of the man is essential, and G.S. Balram Gupta complains that there is not 'even a single authentic biographical-critical study of Anand comprehensive enough to cover all the aspects of his multi-faceted genius'. This is true, though there may be one now that he is dead. Anand's massive fictionalized autobiography, *The Seven Ages of Man*, of which he completed only four volumes, has deterred scholars from attempting anything that comes close to a standard biography. With Anand, as with Rousseau, the 'confessional' flows into the novel, and the mixture produces the fictional autobiographies, the *Kunstler-roman*, and kindred types. How much of *The Seven Ages of Man* is fictional and how much factual is a question a biographer must answer. In private conversations Mulk often called the work factual, but in many of his public statements and letters he preferred to term it fictional. How was a biographer to determine what was actual and what was fictional? Circumventing a work of such magnitude while the author was alive and still writing was not a solution.

It is important to bear in mind that though Mulk's abundant talent has many sides, he is first and foremost a writer, a man of imagination, one who cannot be pinned down to facts—for he creates his own facts. Take his visit to the Mahatma to show him his *Untouchable*. No two of his accounts of the visit are exactly the same! He was no doubt caned by the Indian police for breaking a curfew, but the number of strokes he received often varies from one telling to another. He once told me that Hutchinson International (the original publishers) sold 50,000 copies of *Private Life of an Indian Prince* in paperback. I searched high and low for a copy, but could find none. Finally, I asked Mulk if he would show me his copy of the Hutchinson paperback. He laughed!

The lack of an authentic biography has led scholars to turn to Anand for information. The letters they have received are no doubt valuable, and R.C.P. Yadav in 'Mulk Raj Anand in Letters' expresses the gratitude of many of us to the author. But the inherent danger of being indebted to one's subject and thus being influenced by him is there. Not that such influence is necessarily for the worse. Still a critic must maintain his independence, irrespective of the question of right or wrong. Was it D.H. Lawrence who said that the job of the critic is to save the work from the author! Anand is not the best judge of his own works. Indeed, no author is.

Among notable studies of individual novels in this anthology are Raihan Raza's 'Anand's *Seven Summers*—An Analytical

Study', G.L. Goutam's 'Post-colonial Discourses in Conrad's *Heart of Darkness* and Anand's *Two Leaves and a Bud*' and Syed Afroz Ashrafi's 'The Subaltern Strain in *Untouchable*'. Each study goes beyond the critical examination of the novel concerned to show its wider significance or to place it in context with other works of a similar vein. *Seven Summers* becomes a seminal work when approached with the view of understanding the author's mind and the autobiographical strands that run through his fiction. *Two Leaves and a Bud* (1937), gathers unsuspected depth and meaning when read alongside the anti-colonial masterpiece that is *Heart of Darkness* (1902), and *Untouchable*, already with several firsts, seeks recognition as being also the first of the Dalit novels which have become fashionable today.

This volume has been greatly enriched by three splendid essays, each a specimen of sound scholarship and clarity of thought and expression. A.S. Dasan, one of Anand's most versatile critics, gives an insightful look at Mulk's enormous contribution to the understanding of the arts of India and Asia like music, dance, painting, sculpture, architecture, and frescoe. His 'Anand as a Connoisseur of the Arts' also lends support to Jasbir Jain's sensitively articulated essay, 'Ethical Revolutionaries: The Generation of the Thirties', in which she argues 'the need to see Anand's work in totality, for he was a man who valued "wholeness".' Such a study must, however, come from her, considering her knowledge of the thirties, and her clear-headed approach to Anand's 'humanism'. Tutun Mukherjee in 'Writing as Activism' traces sympathetically the influences of people and events that shaped Anand's thinking, and made him the committed writer he eventually became. She gives several reasons for Anand's loss of readership and painful neglect, and I wouldn't quarrel with them overmuch. But I think it was the lack of an experienced publisher/editor that cost Mulk the most.

A powerful, though none too meticulous writer, Anand needed the careful editing which his London publishers provided him but which was largely absent in India. The publishers he encountered in India, far from correcting any of the author's mistakes in the typescript, added a few of their own while setting the typescript to print. Providing an objective assessment of a work to its author was totally beyond any of them. I remember a publisher once coming to me with the unusual request that I should cut out 40 pages from a new book Mulk had given him, as its present length made its publication uneconomical. 'I can't do that,' I said. 'Mulk will kill me.' 'No, he won't,' replied the publisher with a twinkle in his eyes. 'I won't tell him.'

Though there has been a decline in Anand's estate (he died intestate, leaving trustees and relatives bickering over possession that he had earmarked for charity), there has been a sharp increase in his reputation as a writer. Penguin Books, who had published *Untouchable* and *Coolie* during his lifetime, added three more of his titles to their fiction list in the eighteen months following his death. Critical studies on him are appearing everywhere, and students in Britain, Canada and the United States consider him a safe bet for a research degree. As the world grows more violent, and people less tolerant of one another, his reputation seems to rise phoenix-like because of the abiding values he cherished and upheld.

Saros Cowasjee
University of Regina, Regina
Canada 2007

Acknowledgements

I thank Professor Saros Cowasjee for giving me the permission to include Dolly Sahair's piece entitled 'Mulk's Day in Khandala'. This piece was first published in Mulk Raj Anand's book *Seven Summers: A Memoir* which was edited by Saros Cowasjee. The book was published in 2005 with the Penguin Books.

I am grateful to the prestigious English daily newspaper *The Hindu* for giving me the permission to include the memoir 'The Fall of a Titan' written by Professor Shiv K. Kumar. This memoir was first published in 'The Literary Review' magazine of *The Hindu* on November 7, 2004.

I thank Professor K.K. Sharma for giving me the permission to include Professor G.S. Balram Gupta's paper 'Towards a Closer Understanding of Anand', which was first published in 1977 in the book edited by Prof. K.K. Sharma.

I also express my gratitude towards Atlantic Publishers and Distributors (P) Ltd. for bearing with me patiently. I am happy to be associated with them as their readership is best placed to carry forward the spirit of this book.

And my greatest thanks are reserved to all my contributors, whose help and guidance remained with me throughout. Working so closely with this group of Anand admirers and researchers was a pleasure as well as privilege, and never a job.

Md. Rizwan Khan

Contents

Introduction

When I thought of bringing out a book on Mulk Raj Anand the first thing that came to my mind was to pay tribute to the great master. Therefore, my first and foremost desire has been to create a platform through this book where different types of readers and admirers of Anand will have a chance to talk about their very own Anand which they extracted while reading, interacting or critically evaluating Anand. Usually, when an editor introduces his book, he acknowledges various contributors at the end of his discussion, but I am so overwhelmed with the response and support of my contributors that I cannot postpone the pleasure of talking about their wonderful overtures any further.

Right in the very beginning we were inundated with articles and scholarly write-ups from the whole country. I felt elated to see that Indian literati are so keen to express and share their very own Anand through their academic efforts. I appreciate this with utmost sincerity and thank all my contributors. I would like to specially talk about Professor Shiv K. Kumar, Professor Meenakshi Mukherjee, Professor Saros Cowasjee, Professor Dasan, Professor Jasbir Jain, Professor Balram Gupta and Professor Tutun Mukherjee in this regard. Needless to say, that all these great scholars have enriched the studies in literature through their novel efforts. Owing to their great commitment to their work it was really very difficult for them to squeeze out any moment for a favour to me. But I express this with an indebted heart that not only did all of them come forward promptly to work with me on this project but also gave their invaluable suggestions, guidance and blessings besides their magnificent articles and write-ups. All the contributions to the book have provided me the expected joy and have made me achieve the desired aim as I personally feel that there is this great need to treasure Anand's humane literary world because of its soothing sense of inspiration and positivity cast upon the stark realities of society.

In this world of sordid materialism where literature too has become one of the mere manifestations of the artificiality and superficiality of the post-modern ethos, writers like Anand stand out as prophets of peace, harmony, magnificence, beauty, humanity and traditionality. To talk of a littérateur in these terms while writing in the post-modern literary world may sound clichéd and outdated to the ears used to listening to the quintessentially critical criticism full of pedantic parades, morose attitude, hopeless insight and humiliating interpretations done in the name of rationality, clarity and honesty. One just can't help marvelling at the doyen of Indian English writing and finding him an amalgam of the aforesaid notions which are so innately present in his work that even the so-called rational, clear and honest post-modern criticism finds it too daunting to sever them, as is impossible to separate musicality from a perfect piece of Mozart's symphony. The value of Anand's oeuvre also lies in it being rich and intrinsic in appeal and being powerful enough to make his readers enlightened so much so that they sit back and think. By now, through numerous critiques the intentions in Anand's works are quite obvious. Anand is basically a novelist of the subjects and the motives. He takes up his commitment present in his multitude of experiences related to the reality as a moral responsibility to spread concern.

The Anandian kaleidoscope is comprised of innumerable hues and shades of humanity. Anand comes very close to Prem Chand with regard to the choice of his subjects. Like a painter he paints the land and the people as they are, with a fond stroke of affection in his heart for them, and with a sweeping backdrop of the grime of the universe. This canvas, comprising the dexterous strokes, is framed with the motive, aimed to be achieved through immense sincerity in every single word penned down by Mulk Raj Anand. The motives in Anand's works can be encapsulated in just one term, i.e. concern. Anand has been ascribed to generate the concern for the varied problems that human beings come across in life with a sincere desire to seek solutions to these problems and he is entitled to a fresh veneration from the literary world for this indigenous thematic notion. Anand not only draws attention towards the problems of the marginalized people of the society but also gives an immaculate account with pictorial details of the disgusting chores they have to attend to. Anand has said: "The characters began to compel me to write them out" (Sinha 1989, 19). Thus, Anand the humanist works through his writings to talk about those aspects of common human life, which need concern of the society. It is like a reflection of the pain that hurts Anand himself and becomes too overweening to be ignored. Thus, it is Anand's own consciousness as part of a civilized set-up, which finds its way out through the themes taken up by him in his writings. Anand had undoubtedly a deep desire to search the truth of life and therefore this process of search brought him close to various intellectuals and thinkers. To use his own words: "I grew up in a small world, materially poor, spiritually confined and limited, a world whose narrow boundaries were only trespassed by my inordinate curiosity" (19). He went through the works of Mazzini, Proudhon, Gorky, Marx and Engels to surfeit the curiosity. But it was his own experiences and his own encounters with real life, which gave him the understanding: "I turned in on myself, feeding upon my own life-blood in the obscure lanes and alleys of towns and villages and reaching out beyond myself" (20). This provided him further satiation along with the moral basis of his character. He found this enlightenment dismantling to make him a nonconformist, rebel and visionary.

He disliked the farcical conformations and the compromises needed to be made to become a part of the wise strata. During his stay for the award of a Fellowship in London, Anand got the opportunity to know more about his search. His first encounter with a catastrophe came in the wake of the general strike of coal miners in Britain. The deplorable conditions which the miners lived in touched his heart and at the same time he came across an article written by Karl Marx for the *New York Tribune* in 1853, which had an account of the British imperialist domination of India. By this time Anand's searching soul had got a direction in the form of a missionary zeal and he decided to redress reality through art. *Untouchable* and *Coolie* set him on the path of a lifelong adventure. His commitment to humanism made him drift away from the British intellectuals with whom he was disillusioned for their not having "centrality of vision". He was close to writers like Lowes Dickinson and E.M. Forster. Later on, he converted to Marxism adhering fully to the Marxist doctrine: *It is not the consciousness of men that determines their existence but, on the contrary, it is their social existence that determines their consciousness.* Under the influence of Tolstoy, Morris, Ruskin and Gandhi, Anand further strengthened his adherence to a moderate socialism. Despite all this, Anand never committed himself to any political affiliation. The artist in him only got the aesthetic strength from the humanist in him and never got distracted from the motives in his works. Jawahar Lal Nehru, the greatest humanist of India had a strong influence on him. To quote M.C. Pant "His concern with Nehru, and the things associated with that name are cardinal principles of faith with him" (23).

Anand's motives in his work are not only to highlight the problems and miseries but he also meticulously makes an effort to suggest the ways out of them. Anand was a Nehruvian socialist committed to the building up of the nation at a time in history, which was a very vulnerable stage of freshly achieved freedom. The humanist in Anand had taken it upon himself to seek, to strive and to fight for the restoration of a society, free from the prejudices and discriminations. He talks of the casteism, rich-poor drift, problems of the women who are subject to gender discrimination, problems of those who face economic depravity, and problems of those who are psychologically suffering at one level or the other. Anand has a plethora of concerns but all have common motive surging behind, i.e. to let the common human beings come up with a resistance against the hardships of their life. Anand's approach is not like that of Renaissance humanism, which just theorizes the betterment of human life, but he is very realistic in his visionary dispositions about the betterment of the human beings.

Anand's motives in the humanist literary endeavors are novel because he creates an aura of grandeur and dignity in the struggles, which his characters undergo. The essential zeal of dignity bestowed on the characters in their respective struggles is marked in almost all the major protagonists like Bakha, Munoo, Bhikhu, Gangu, Ananta and Maqbool. Every character comes up with a dignified satisfaction in his individual fights. Every human being in this world has his own set of problems. These problems get aggravated when factors like class, caste, creed, race, colour, religion and sex too join in. In such circumstances an individual stands out because of his improvisations lent to the situation to come up with a sense of pride typically characteristic of human nature. There is no gainsaying the fact that the atrocities, with which the characters in Anand's works are subjected to, are not atypical; but Anand simply makes his people excel in their show of the dignity, which is imbibed in their resistance to the oppression and adversities. This is because of the reason that Anand respects each and every oppressed soul as a distinct individual; each one capable enough with a will power to carve out a niche for himself as a willing human being. He does not delineate his characters with a sweeping account of condescending philosophical concerns; rather he lets every individual grow on his own in a manner belonging only to him and no one else, guided by self-esteem and self-respect. But at the same time these characters are inspired from some or the other precedent and do establish a precedent for others too.

In *Untouchable*, the three solutions: religious conversion, change of the mindset of the society and flush sanitary system reflect Anand's missionary and socialist zeal to eradicate untouchability. *Coolie* provides an exploration of the limits of pain, central to existence. Munoo a weak and helpless person is subjected to a degrading society offering only hostility. But, here also it is not the ultimate tragedy that holds forth the centre.

In fact, this one puts forth an individual's ways of surviving amidst despair and degradation involving primitivism, capitalism, industrialism, communalism and colonialism and here it is not just an external strength that is the concern but Munoo's subdued undercurrent of delight comes up as a mode of internal strength to provide a way out and thus Munoo emerges out as an admirable character for his humane and hedonistic impulses. The novel *Two Leaves and a Bud* is concentrated on the analysis of colonialism. The backdrop of tea plantation portrays the inhumanity and the might of the British Empire. The main protagonist Gangu undergoes an awesome battle with a life full of anger, cries and crime with no sympathy at all. Though apparently the cruelty and oppression seem to be victorious, the novel extracts power from the 'counter pointing of good and evils'. The novel, often viewed as a moral allegory, comes out to be the one comprising dream and delight. The protagonists in all these three novels emerge out to be fighters though not with much success, even then relentless, owing to their desire for the betterment. Thus, Anand's motive is witnessed in the effort to retain the essential positivism based on the resolute attitude of the simple human beings.

The trilogy has much stronger protagonists who are avowed to get the energy released, which is arrested with the protagonists of the first three novels. There is a swing towards delight as the hero's involvement and determination is profound towards the path of Anandian motive. *The Village* exhibits a conflict between the adolescent and the adult world. Though the protagonist leaves his country with a heavy heart and at an unhappy turn of events in his life yet there is hope in the fact that he is embarking on a journey to another country and thus there is a future in store for him, full of uncertainties but definitely with a scope for betterment and change. *Across the Black Waters* deals with the futility of war. The war takes over as the main concern and one confronts the graduated experiences of the protagonist. Anand foregrounds the macrocosmic catastrophe of the human world through the war and the protagonist perseveres his way out. The third novel of the trilogy, *The Sword and the Sickle* deals with a further graduation in the journey of the experiences of Lal Singh whereby projecting him in a political backdrop and involved in painful strife between revolution and his love. A mature Lal Singh resists, with a conviction, to emerge as a complete and resolute individual. Anand's motive is to show the class struggle and to offer a solution in the ways of Lal Singh's efforts.

The Big Heart delineates Ananta's battle against the hackneyed concepts of his community and against the owners of machines, Lala Murli Dhar and Gokul Chand, who exploit the workers. The novel has strong thematic emanations related to the socialist concern of Anand. The struggle ensuing between "haves" and "have-nots" and interests of selfish individuals do not diminish the protagonists' positive belief that a new life has to be created. Anand envisages a solution through Ananta that the new life will have machines as the usherers of sufficiency, wealth and love.

Seven Summers and *Private Life of an Indian Prince* do not come directly in the line of Anand's socialist and missionary motives but are definitely depictions of Anand's humanist zeal. The autobiographical *Seven Summers* captures a child—Anand's raw, vital, innocent, pleasant, sensitive, sensuous and desirous imaginations recollected in a nostalgic mood. A child at such a tender age normally does not receive serious concern for his thirst for experience and encouragement for his novel ideas, although it is the formative part of his life. Therefore, it is a sort of social marginalization which tends to create realistic and essential bitterness in the child. Anand, by taking up such delineation aims to share the concern related to a child's innocent world. *Private Life of an Indian Prince* is a work of serious psychological contours extracted in the portrayal of the protagonist. There is no effort to create an etching of life in its profundities. There is an attempt on Anand's part to venture into an entirely different genre of fiction that is about the child psychology.

The novels, *The Old Woman and the Cow, The Road* and *Death of a Hero* witness the resurgence of the characteristic Anandian humanist concern with strong motives and resolute convictions. The *Old Woman and the Cow* explores the dimensions of a woman's life grasping the modern fictional experiment. Gauri's ordeal is nothing new to talk about, for a woman, but it is the modern day Sita who hits out, but without Rama. Gauri undergoes exploitation at the hands of her husband, mother and others but she fights hard to safeguard her chastity. She does not meet Sita's end though she is in the same situation as Sita was and here comes a harbinger's spirit when she moves on in her life taking up a job as a nurse and discards her husband. Anand phenomenally extracts out the strength and life force in Gauri's character by transforming her weak stature into the one full of resolution and conviction. He motivates a suggestion of economic self-reliance as one of the ways to come out of the age-old sufferings and exploitations—emotional as well as physical—for women.

Anand again takes up an untouchable's story in *The Road*. The novel is a landmark in the journey of Anand's meticulous effort for the redemption of the society from its ills. Bhikhu, the protagonist, is an untouchable and a crusader. The novel is the perfect explication of Anand's commitment to redress reality through art. Bhikhu's struggle is mental, physical and social. He takes up a Herculean job of constructing a road to the city despite the serious opposition from the upper castes. Anand enthuses the protagonist with a sheer desire to stand up against all odds and relentlessly surge ahead towards a better social status. The road built is not only a solution in material terms to take the people to the city, out of economic depravity, but also a harbinger of change which leads Bhikhu finally to a city where untouchability does not prevail. The motive in *The Road* is to bring out a solution from within and not from without as Bhikhu the untouchable individually takes it upon himself to crusade against untouchability.

Death of a Hero deals with Maqbool Sherwani's ways of resistance and restoring, with the issues of general concern. The tribal invaders from across the border are given a tough fightback by the people who are enthused with the glorious patriotism of Maqbool Sherwani. Anand's portrayal is a very novel one in that it frames the contemporary problem in the solution guided by classical and mythical values. Maqbool

Sherwani's poetry, valour, zealous adventurism, fantastic pragmatism and selflessness are committed to serve the humanist cause, i.e. to safeguard the nation and the national interest. His mannerisms to reach his goal reflect a reaffirmed faith in the age-old heroic notions, which in the modern world, one often tends to relate only with the fantasy. He lays down his life and becomes a crucified patriot who even questions if there is any God who would just helplessly watch the weak suffer. He endorses Jesus Christ's ways of serving the humanity and thus is a prophetic protagonist in the Anandian plethora of harbingers. Here, Anand has reached a pinnacle in his journey for the search of solutions to the problems of humanity.

Anand's fiction reinstates the basic expectations from art. At a time in history when every single choice was a luxury in the country and literature too was expected to serve some purpose like other institutions to the contemporary needs, Anand marched ahead and tried to carve out a niche for his artistic zeal and for his insatiate thirst of concern. The present-day crises in the modern predicament, which has lent uncertainty, lack of direction, hopelessness and intolerance to the human value-system, need to be addressed through the ways, which Anand explicates in his works. The institutions of human value system are seeking fresh testimonials from their canons as the topsy-turvy holds forth. In a way these canons exist in the works of Anand. One can always bank on the solidity provided by Anand's motives (concern and solution). It's time to take up a revitalized attempt to go through the works of Anand in order to find a way out because one needs to hold on to some centre which is potent with the power to uproot the anarchy—the anarchy in the form of culture and habit of the society—which guards the jaded hypocrisy in the name of customs, class, religion and values. This jaded hypocritical behaviour needs an unrelenting, interminable and eternal fightback, which is sufficiently inculcated through the Anandian motives.

This book is presented to the readers with sincere intentions aimed at revoking a spirited endeavor towards studies in Anand because Anand's works not only are precious pieces of literature, but also the texts full of pragmatic humanism and are deeply rooted in energy capable of achieving the progress much needed. The great Urdu poet and Anand's one of the mentors, Iqbal (1992) has said:

Utho meri duniya ke gharibon ko jaga do
Kaakh-e-umaraa ke dar-o-deewar hila do (401)

* * *

Jis khet se dehqan ko mayassar nahi rozi
Us khet ke har khosha-e-gandum ko jala do (402)

(Rise and awake the slumbering poor with your clarion call,
Pull down the palaces, shake their doors and walls.)
(Singe the stalks of wheat and rice, burn down the fields,
Which can't provide the peasant with his daily needs.)

(Kanda 19)

These couplets perfectly reflect the themes and spirit of Anand and his works.

REFERENCES

Iqbal, Allama. *Kulliyat–e–Iqbal.* K.C. Kanda (trans.). New Delhi: New Dawn Press, 2006.

Sinha, K.N. *Mulk Raj Anand*, New Delhi – Ludhiana: Kalyani Publishers, 1989.

MEMORIES

Fall of a Titan*

1

Shiv K. Kumar

Uncle Mulk is no more. The last outpost has fallen on the darkling plain after the passing away of R.K. Narayan, Dom Moraes and Nissim Ezekiel. Honoured with the Padma Bhushan, the Sahitya Akademi and several other International awards, Mulk Raj Anand will always be remembered as the doyen of Indian English writers, spanning about seven decades. He was "uncled" by many young writers because he offered his generous patronage to every new literary aspirant. He was not like most other celebrities who are often niggardly in recognizing new talent.

Authentic Articulation

Mulk Raj Anand felt catapulted into literary fame by E.M. Forster's glowing foreword to his novel *Untouchable* (1935), followed by *Coolie* (1936) and a string of both novels and collections of short stories: *Across the Black Waters, Two Leaves and a Bud, The Sword and the Sickle* and *Confessions of a Lover*. His forte lay in articulating authentic emotion; because most of his fictional writing was structured around intensely felt personal experiences.

Like Khushwant Singh, he was not a believer. To him God was a teaser whose dispensations were capricious, unjust and irrational. The genesis of Mulk's agnosticism might be traced to his shock, at the age of 11, over the death of his nine-year-old cousin, Kaushalya. This provoked him into writing a letter to God asking, "why He had taken Kaushalya away". This letter

---

* This paper was first published in 'Literary Review', *The Hindu*, November 7, 2004.

was presumably his first piece of writing and in it, Mulk found his voice as an agnostic. Later on, his agnosticism was deepened in *The Grand Inquisitor*, a scene in *Brothers Karamazov*. So it was this curious mix between denial and Marxism, which awakened him to the predicament of the labouring classes in his own country.

Role of Creativity

In the early 1950s, Mulk and I entered into a spirited argument over the function of creative writing. In an aricle I wrote in 1955 on progressive writers, I had, somewhat harshly, dismissed such political literature as mere rhetoric and propaganda. I had also quoted a couplet by Iqbal, a poet Mulk admired very much. It said:

Agar kajroh hain anjum
Asman tera hai ya mera
Mujhe fikre jehan kyon ho
Jehan tera hai ya mera
(If the stars have gone awry,
the sky is yours, not mine.
Why should I lend myself to angst
When the universe is yours, not mine?)

To this Mulk reacted quite sharply, in a letter dated November 6, 1955:

> May I ask, however, why you denigrate the obsession of these Indian writers with underdogs? Does not 80 per cent at least of the population of our country live in the most sordid and abject poverty? And are the writers merely to wish away the social and human cause...?

These words certainly unhinged my critical stance and I confessed to him my misjudgment. Indeed, I always lauded Mulk's forthright convictions, which sprang from a genuine transparency. As I now look at his letters, written to me over the past four decades,—letters humane or strident, compassionate or pungent—I notice that he never wrote with malice towards anyone, even when his words sometimes sounded somewhat harsh.

Let me share with the readers his incisive assessments of Salman Rushdie, V.S. Naipaul, Nirad Chaudhuri and Ruth Prawer Jhabvala. In his letter of August 7, 1982, he wrote:

> The question of Salman Rushdie's novel does not arise as far as I am concerned. Rushdie is a clever young man (perhaps too clever by half as the English say). He writes very eloquently in the English language but in *Midnight's Children*, he is aping the recent Americans by disemboweling his mother, painting his grandmother as a scheming old witch, his grandfather as a burglar, his father as a mere crook, and he himself as superior to all his colleagues. I suppose he is brighter than the others, but in the kind of way in which the average advertising copywriter is brighter than every other copywriter. India appears to be a spittoon to Salman Rushdie. I suppose it is as it was a vast sewage to Katherine Mayo before the war, or it is the "Continent of Circe" to that third grade actor Nirad Chaudhuri, as it is "An Area of Darkness" to V.S. Naipaul, as it is "Heat and Dust" to Ruth Jhabvala....

Nor does he spare Aurobindo in this letter of May 20, 1987:

> I don't deny intellectual apperceptions to Sri Aurobindo, but the Miltonic epic style can only express itself in rounded statements. Blake was also a mystic, but knew the contraries....

Comprehending Reality

Mulk Raj Anand implies that unless a poet can confront the complexities of life, its incoherencies and paradoxes, he cannot comprehend reality in its entirety. This ironic mode of perception is, therefore, the only way to understand the tension at the heart of poetic craft.

In another letter (April 5, 1986), Mulk perceives death as an inevitable end to human existence. When he had a stroke in that year, I wrote to him in fear and trembling. In response, he said:

> I am moved by your concern for me. Actually it was a false alarm.... But you know, my dear Shiv, that decay

> is inevitable at eighty. But I am fighting it, if only to say my say.

His panacea for overcoming the dread of extinction lay in returning to his writing:

> For three hours, from 6.00 to 9.00 in the morning (I write) and, of course, the cycle of pain and pleasure, gets mixed up into the Christian cross, all for Art, since I am finishing the 3rd part of the 5th volume of the confessional, and so He Played His Part.

Like Dostoevsky, he believed that a writer discovers himself in his creations and that he has no other vocation.

Mulk Raj Anand's death has indeed created a vacuum in contemporary Indian English writing that will not be filled for many years to come. We are now left mostly with literature that is loaded with sex and violence, traits that never tainted the work of R.K. Narayan, Raja Rao and Mulk Raj Anand—the illustrious triumvirate of yesteryears.

Call Me Uncle Mulk

2

Meenakshi Mukherjee

My first meeting with Mulk Raj Anand was a disaster. The year was 1968 and the place Mysore. For some years I had been reading Anand avidly in connection with my doctoral research and was about to present a paper on some aspect of his work at what was probably the first ever conference on Indian Writing in English to be held in the country. With an unfinished Ph.D. and hardly any publication to my name I had no qualification to be part of that august gathering. I was there mostly on sufferance—largely due to the legendary kindness of Professor C.D. Narasimhaiah towards young aspirants. When I arrived at the University Guest House the evening before the conference and looked at the programme, my heart sank. Had I known that the subject of my paper would be present I would certainly have organized my argument differently.

Even after more than three decades, I still remember vividly all the details of that fateful encounter. In my paper I had attempted a comparative study of Mulk Raj Anand's Lalu trilogy and a tetralogy written by Sudhin Ghose, a writer whose use of fantasy and myth fascinated me. Both sets of novels were about the growing up of an adolescent, but the narrative styles of the writers were diametrically opposite. I was trying to be objective while contrasting the social realist mode of Anand with the whimsical non-realist (the term 'magic realism' had not been invented then) mode of Ghose, but my preference for the latter was not very well concealed. With youthful brashness I had argued that obliqueness had an edge over direct representation in fiction. The paper had already been submitted and copies put in the conference folder of each participant.

There was no way I could have now modified my views or deflect the focus.

Next morning while presenting the paper I tried my best to tone down the argument a little—punctuating the paper with 'perhaps', 'one way of looking at it', 'some might think' and other such modifiers. But my damage control exercise did not work. A visibly upset Mulk Raj Anand stood up after my paper and wanted to know who I was. He rebuked me for my total lack of literary judgment and wondered how someone so ignorant was allowed to read a paper. He reminded the audience that his novels had been translated into eighteen languages in the world and questioned the right of this young upstart here to criticize his work. I was completely devastated, and although the rest of the day I forced myself to sit through the paper reading sessions, I was too stunned to take anything in. It was my first seminar participation and I was pretty sure that it was going to be my last as well.

In the evening I was sitting alone in my Guest House room nursing my bruised ego, too embarrassed to go out and socialize with the other participants. There was a knock on the door and I could not believe my eyes when I found the great novelist himself standing outside. Mulk Raj Anand put his hand on my shoulder and told me gently: "I am sorry. I was rude to you this morning. Please forgive me. Call me Uncle Mulk and kiss me on the cheek."

In later life after I got to know him better, I have often thought that my first meeting with him captured the essence of Mulk Raj Anand's personality—impulsive as well as generous, self-absorbed yet warm and compassionate. My second meeting with him was some five years later in Delhi. By that time, my doctoral dissertation had come out as a book titled *The Twice-born Fiction* but I had no idea that Anand had read it. He was giving a public lecture at the India International Centre, and I was sitting at the back of the auditorium. At the end of his lecture, he was presented with a bouquet of flowers. He got up and said—"Don't give it to me! Give it to that critic of mine sitting there in the last row. She knows more than I do. Her book will tell you what is wrong with my work." Obviously, he had not forgiven me yet. This time, however, I was not quite sure what my offence was. In the book, I tried to be much more balanced and fair than I had been in the Mysore paper. But perhaps Anand thought I was not enthusiastic enough about his literary achievements.

In December 1977, a huge conference was held in Delhi—the 4th Triennial of ACLALS (Association for Commonwealth Literature and Language Studies) under the Chairmanship of Professor C.D. Narasimhaia. It was my first international conference and meeting in person writers and critics from across the world whose names I had so far seen only in print, was quite a heady experience. In retrospect, I think one memorable feature of the conference was not listed in the programme. There were informal open air lunchtime meetings in the golden sunshine of Delhi winter. At least three literary gurus held court under separate trees. Raja Rao wore what was described in a newspaper report as "his batman robe"—a loose black cloak. His devotees sat at his feet with their lunch plates perched on their knees. Under another tree was the enigmatic G.V. Desani, whose *All About H. Hatterr* had by that time assumed an iconic status. Mulk Raj Anand was the centre of a third group. Some non-aligned participants like me flitted from the periphery of one to the other. When Mulk Raj Anand caught sight of me, he called me and made a request: "Will you please come to the screening of my film 'The Lost Child' this evening?" Many things were happening simultaneously at each session of the conference but I was so flattered by Anand's special invitation that I dropped everything and travelled across the city to be present at the screening. It was a beautiful film and after the screening was over I went up to him to tell him how moved I was. "So you don't think I am an old fool after all." He said with a twinkle in his eyes.

In subsequent years, I kept meeting Anand at irregular intervals—in Delhi, Mumbai, Jodhpur, Mysore and other places and his half-bantering digs at my work continued. He told me his life story several times over—his humble beginnings in Punjab, his gestation period in England and his return to the country to work on several fronts at the same time: art, literature and social action. He told me I would be able to understand his novels better only if I saw the larger background. Indeed his involvement with the public issues of our time was something that interested me increasingly. We were in Jodhpur right after the infamous self-immolation case of Roop Kanwar, and Anand's keynote speech there was an angry indictment of the people who aided and abetted the act and glorified it afterwards. Within a few hours he received an anonymous letter of threat: he would have to pay dearly if he did not stay out of the cultural and religious matters of Rajasthan which he as an outsider would never understand. Undaunted, he returned to the same topic in an intervention the next day. I admired his courage of conviction. I have high regard for Anand in his role of a public intellectual and the positions he took on communalism and religious fundamentalism. But that was not enough. He insisted that I write again of his novels and revise my early assessment.

My last encounter with him was in the late nineties in Delhi when Suresh Kohli was making a Sahitya Akademi-sponsored film on Mulk Raj Anand. Kohli rang up one day and said "Mulk wants a five-minute conversation with you to be part of the film". "Most certainly", I said, "I am honoured. Tell me where I should come, and when." "No, he would like to come to your place." I was delighted but I reminded Suresh Kohli that we lived on the second floor and there was no lift in the building. But that did not deter Anand. He still had boundless energy and the steep stairs seemed to have had no effect on him. He arrived with the camera crew who started moving furniture, putting the telephone off the hook and generally playing havoc with whatever order existed in our household. They made Anand and me sit on two chairs next to each other and ordered: 'Start'. Exactly on cue, Mulk Raj Anand began his life story and I tried to look as attentive as possible. In a minute or two the camera crew shouted 'cut, cut'. I was not sure what was wrong but after a while they asked us to start again. Unfazed, Anand began again at the beginning and went through the story exactly in the same way until the camera crew shouted 'cut' once more. This sequence of 'cut' and 'start' went on a few times and at some point I began to wonder what exactly my role was. Should

I not say something to make it sound like a conversation? But it was not easy to put in a word edgeways. The flow of his autobiographical narration was so exuberant that no intervention was possible at any point.

I had forgotten about the film until Suresh Kohli called again after a few months. “Mulk wants you to come to a preview of the film at Hauz Khas Village.” It was a small studio and the audience consisted of Anand, Kohli, myself and a friend, who had come with me. I had gone with high expectations, hoping to have some glimpses of his earlier life—at least a few still photographs from his youth in London with his friends like Sajjad Zaheer and the group who used to meet in the backroom of Nanking Restaurant to write the first draft of the manifesto of the All India Progressive Writers Conference. May be even a few stray pictures with the Bloomsbury writers he came to be in touch with. But the film did not delve much into the archives. It consisted mostly of Mulk Raj Anand’s long ‘conversations’ with various people, conducted in the last few months. At places Anand’s speech seemed blurred. When the screening was over, there were a few minutes of silence. Then Anand turned to me and said “Meenakshi, tell me honestly, what do you think of the film?” I was at a loss for words and hesitantly answered, “Perhaps it could be edited a little.” Anand faced Suresh with an ‘I-told-you-so’ look and said “Exactly. Some of the conversations have to be done again. My old dentures did not fit.”

I have not seen the final version of the film. We left Delhi to move to Hyderabad soon after and did not have a chance to meet Mulk Raj Anand again. The day in November 2004 the newspapers reported his departure, one of the papers also carried in the op-ed page an article by Anand that came to them a few days ago. Perhaps he had dictated it from his sick-bed. I wish I had preserved that cutting. As I recall now it had to do with the Best Bakery case—or something else relating to the post-Godhra inquiry. At ninety-nine, he was still capable of being agitated over matters of public ethics. This is the Uncle Mulk I shall always remember with admiration and affection—one who did not “go gentle into the good night”. Till the end he “rage[d] against the dying of light”.

Mulk's Day in Khandala*

3

Dolly Sahair

As always, Mulk wakes up at 5 a.m. Earlier he would have gone for a walk, but that he can no longer do. He has his bath and gets ready for the day.

His day begins with tea and three Shrewsberry biscuits. He insists on writing—at least a few lines. We give him his writing board and ruled paper. He sits contemplating for a while, staring at the blank sheet before him. Then he scribbles, scratches it out, and scribbles again. 'What are you writing, Mulk?' I ask him. 'Autobiographical saga', is the answer I get.

After his stint at writing, he loves to sit in the garden and feel the warm sun on his face. Sometimes we go to the edge of the compound, from where we can see the sparkling stream and the little pool in the valley below. In days gone by, we often went down to the pool for a swim, and then there was the long climb back the cottage. The memory of it is ever fresh in our minds.

Sitting in the garden, I would try to make him talk. I find it strange that a man who had so much to say has now gone silent. I would read him the headlines from the daily *Asian Age*. He would listen attentively, and if anything caught his interest, he would make me read the whole news story.

Soon it would be time for breakfast. Breakfast with him is a simple affair, but it is the time when a friend or a visitor might drop in to greet him. Occasionally, students doing research on

---

* This short piece was first published in *Seven Summers: A Memoir,* edited by Saros Cowasjee in 2005 with Penguin Books. This piece was written by Dolly Sahair for Saros Cowasjee.

his works would come for help. Though unable to give them the time he once did, he listens to them patiently and answers their questions as best as he can. People who visit him often forget how old he is—they still look on him as the vigorous man he was in his eighties!

Mulk must have his nap. Somewhere between 11.30 and 12 noon, he retires to his room for two hours. He then has lunch which consists of dal, rice, vegetables and fruits. He is not particular about what food you serve him, but he must have a piece of chocolate. Most of the cooking and cleaning is done by his caregivers (Mulk abhors the word 'servent'), who adore him. Mulk has a great capacity for commanding affection and there is not a thing they would not do for him. I am never afraid of leaving Mulk alone with them during my regular visits to Bombay.

When I am in Khandala, it has been my practice to read to him for an hour or more after he has had his lunch. It may be a travelogue which would remind him of his own various travels, or it could be excerpts from one of his novels. He likes to hear his own words, especially from his autobiographies like *Morning Face* and *Confessions of a Lover*. Often his face lights up and he nods his head approvingly. It is important that someone should be there to read to Mulk, and I have got two young boys to read to him in my absence. One of them reads to him in Hindi.

Mulk was always very punctilious in replying to letters, but the task proves too much for him now. I read him letters (he has a huge mail!), and sometimes he tells me what I should write. But there are times when he says nothing, and then the letters go unanswered. It can't be helped. Many of those who write to Mulk have not seen him for years and do not know that he is too frail to reply.

As evening approaches, Mulk looks forward to his favourite treat-brandy with honey, lemon and hot water. It is a must. He has had it for the past 50 years that I have known him, and no day is complete without it.

The last event of the day is the BBC news on television at about 7.30 p.m. Sometimes he might stay up to watch a cricket match or a documentary with his caregivers. At 9 p.m., he retires to bed, and that marks the end of a normal day in the life of Mulk at the age of ninety-nine.

You can see there is not much happening outwardly now. But what is taking place in Mulk's mind, none of us know.

DELIBERATIONS

Ethical Revolutionaries: The Generation of the Thirties

4

Jasbir Jain

I first met Mulk Raj Anand in the mid-sixties when I had just begun work on George Orwell and I was building up on my knowledge of Orwell's co-workers in the BBC. Balraj Sahni was another person whom I tapped for his impressions. While Balraj Sahni responded fulsomely, Anand was more in the present. The past was behind him and colonial memories had been overlaid by other aesthetic concerns. Again, at a seminar in Jodhpur, I had the privilege of interacting with him. Anand was the main speaker; his range was wide and perceptions provocative in their sensitivity and newness. His reading and involvement in sculpture and painting, his concern with bridging up the gap between art and life came through.

At some point of time I requested him for a 'Foreword' to my work on Orwell. His response was curt and put me off. He said 'Forewords' were like crutches, which a good scholar should avoid. I was hurt. How unobliging with his own early dependence on 'Forewords'? But later as I saw his 'Forewords' to other books by other writers, it dawned on me that he had paid me a compliment. 'Forewords' eclipse the writer; they are patronising and like a wall. I had learnt my lesson. Thank you, Mr. Anand.

Going through some library catalogues and bibliographies, one is overwhelmed by the sheer quantum of his work, his life long involvement in art and philosophy and his long editorship of Marg. In real life, his eyes were the most alive part of his face. But when I go through the work on him, I am sadly disappointed. The links between his various interests have not yet been sufficiently made. I am grateful to Mohammed Rizwan

Khan for pushing me into this and providing the occasion for a fresh reading of some of Anand's work. This reading has helped clarify some concepts I have been working on—the alternative/new humanism that has emerged in our writing and the category of emotional logic which defeats mere rationalism. There is a need to see Anand's work in its totality for he was a man who valued 'wholeness'.

* * *

Anand wrote his first novel *Untouchable* in 1931 though it took four more years before it could reach the public in 1935. Raja Rao's *Kanthapura* appeared in 1937 and R.K. Narayan's *Swami and Friends* appeared in 1935 to be followed closely by *The Bachelor of Arts* in 1937. But they were not the only writers' representative of the generation of the thirties. There were others both in India and abroad—dissident intellectuals, rebels, bewildered men impatient to act and mould a new world.[1] In India the thirties was a time of turbulence, revolution and unrest. Gandhi's non-cooperation movement of 1921-22 had already happened and the famous Dandi March took place in March 1930. Chandershekhar Azad and Bhagat Singh were to pay with their lives for their revolutionary zeal and resistance to imperial authoritarianism.[2] Subhash Chandra Bose was beginning to fret against Gandhian ideology.[3] And Premchand whose fiction dealt with situations of oppression and social reform addressed the Progressive Writers Movement in 1936.

In England the generation of the thirties had turned towards communism or social thought. A number of them participated in the Spanish Civil War on one side or the other. And others, who did not actually do so, still disaffiliated themselves from the weak liberal humanism of Middleton Murry and his generation, intellectuals who were critical of the Empire but not courageous enough to disown it. Orwell who worked in the BBC Eastern Service from 1940 to 1943, with which Mulk Raj Anand was fairly closely associated, was a loner. Neither did he subscribe to the code of the white man's burden nor to the party line of the left. A non-conformist he straddled the area between liberal humanism and existential thought. Orwell in 1949 wrote an essay on Gandhi, "Reflections on Gandhi", in which he wrote: 'Almost from childhood onwards he had a deep earnestness, an attitude ethical rather than religious...' (CEJL, IV, 465). Gandhi's human sainthood in lesser mortals has been defined as plain and simple 'decency'. Orwellian critics have used this word time and again and the scholarship on Anand has echoes of it in the references to his humanism.

Besides the poets about whom Orwell has written in "Inside the Whale"[4] there were writers like Christopher Isherwood who turned to Eastern thought even as some of them travelled to Europe. This conjunction of ideas, despite the geographical distances, evidenced a world that was possessed with similar notions of ethics, of the self and of freedom. Anand's life and writing both reveal a coming together of the myriad strands of experience, pursuit of knowledge, self-questioning and revolutionary ideology centred on the human being. It is not possible to dismiss his association with Forster and Orwell, or to ignore his fascination with Gandhi or his lifelong preoccupation with art and aesthetics even as it is not possible to dismiss the fact of his being part of the experience of the thirties. The location in history and the expatriate location in 1925 in England right upto the early 40s are equally important.

Orwell had joined the Imperial Police in search of employment, a path his father before him had chosen; Anand went to England to study philosophy as many an Indian before him had done. While Orwell's stay in India turned him into a critic of imperial structures, Anand's in England pushed him into greater involvement with his country's politics. What is it that this distancing from the homeland does to the individual to bring about a transformation in his notion of self and the other?

In my attempt to define Anand's humanism which has been so generously commented upon by scholars, but which has never properly been distinguished from other strands of humanism, I cannot help but trace a genealogy from Gandhian thought working through the diasporic experience in South Africa and leading to Hind Swaraj and its aftermath. In my ongoing engagement with alternative discourses I too have often used the term humanism. For the last few years I have been referring to it as distinct from the white man's humanism which was humanism based on the ideas of colour and race and the western ideas of linear progress. It is only now that I have begun to see the way this alternative humanism is different in its ethics of belief and action and its ethics of equality. The purpose of my present engagement with Anand is to understand the shaping of the writer's ideology and the emerging meaning of humanism. My main reference point is Anand's *Apology for Heroism.*

* * *

Apology for Heroism was written in 1945, the year the Second World War ended. Published the very next year, it went into a second and then a third edition. In his "Preface to the Third Edition" in 1975, Anand wrote that when he wrote it at the end of the war he had already begun to feel that life 'could not be reduced to abstract ideas. All the feelings, which are inbetween the lines, the contraries and the chaos of the human situation, demand the mirror of creative emotion to reflect them'. Having given up his pursuits of professional philosophy, Anand could only call his 'search for faith as the search for human beings, or humanness, or the dignity of weakness in men or women'. Thus, *Apology for Heroism* is a confession of the futility of his earlier pursuit and the false emphasis on the brahminical tradition. In a world of immoralities, man as a moral being can find sustenance only in his own creativeness, in his faith in men and through shifting the emphasis from superficial acts of worship to the worship of humanity. In this he was echoing the Nehruvian goal of 'Destination Man' as well as a critiquing of elitist cultures. In this there was also the need to deconstruct the idea of universalism, which was eurocentric and unequal at its very core. In fact, Anand's working towards a new humanism was a questioning of power and power structures.

In the preface to the first edition in 1945, Anand referred to the work as 'a very tentative introduction to the humanism which I have been evolving for myself through the jig-saw puzzle of my Indian upbringing and my Eur-Asian experience'. The Anandian humanism is a confrontation with the self based not on arrogance and self-assurance but on humility. It also effects a conjunction of two different cultures, a conjunction referred to in different contexts as hybridity (Bhabha), schizophrenia (Sahgal) or a rivening apart, a cleavage (Nirmal Verma).[5] An earlier reflection of this can be seen in Gandhi's *My Experiments with Truth* where the upbringing in a conventional Saurashtrian bania household, as it comes into contact with other cultures, thinkers and experiences, leads to an overwhelming preoccupation with dignity. It was first the experience in England and then in South Africa, which constituted Gandhi's idea of the human. Apparently the clear focus and the distancing which diasporic experience results in push an individual to this questioning of the 'self'.

Despite the fact that some thinkers are of the view that the Indian notion of 'self' does not incorporate any need for the 'other',[6] it needs to be recognized that expatriate experience has been instrumental in the intellectual formation of a nation. Mulk Raj Anand in London and Raja Rao in Paris went through similar experiences reflecting in some measures what Jawaharlal Nehru and Krishna Menon had experienced before them. Raja Rao's *The Meaning of India* reflects on his early formative experiences abroad. But much before any of these Gandhi carried his stubborn resistance to discrimination to its logical extreme in South Africa.[7] Giriraj Kishore's novel *Pahla Girmitiya* and before that Shyam Benegal's film *The Making of the Mahatma* illustrate Gandhi's experiences and responses with conviction. It is here, on a foreign soil, that both the atrocities of imperial power and the need to take a stand on the basis of one's humanity become emphatic. It is also here that a sifting takes place between our past experiences and our present needs. The expatriate first learns to look at himself through the eyes of the others and then through his own eyes. These two images as they confront each other generate their own resolution. This experience is shared by all those who crossover whether it be a Malcolm Muggeridge, an E.M. Forster or a C.F. Andrews.

Humanism is not condescension, nor is it a political ideology. It recognizes the dignity of the other as well as the grandeur of resistance. This recognition erases animosity as well as pity. Anand's humanism had begun at home between with the two different lifestyles of his parents and the secularism they both practised in different ways. His mother placed the Hindu idols 'side by side with a crucifix which she had picked up somewhere, a picture of the Aga Khan, and of Guru Nanak' while his father had inherited 'a family devotion to the peculiar Ismaili religion' (29-30). On this background the Arya Samaj movement was another layer. The opposing strands of imperial control and colonial resistance constituted the social structure in India, one that Indians had to face and live through. His nationalistic impulses, a spell in prison as a Gandhian follower, and a growing attraction for a Muslim girl, were some of the factors, which led to a family quarrel and pushed him into self-exile in 1925. The young Anand writes about his disgust for all kinds of compromises, compromises that subtracted from the legendary Indian ethical values. In England the exposure to the British class reality and the General Strike of 1926 led him further into self-introspection. *Untouchable*, Anand's first novel, expresses his conflicts of this early period. He was barely twenty-five when he wrote it. The different solutions, which Bakha considers in turn, are all a reflection of Anand's concerns with two philosophical traditions—Western and Eastern, the social and economic stratifications prevalent in all societies, and the dignity of a human being. What does it mean to be a man? is the question which dominates his early novels. Religious faith and conversion form one component in *Untouchable*, Gandhian strategy of going across another, technology and the development of the machine a third and a poet's imagination a fourth. It was natural for Anand, after all this self and social questioning, to go back to the Indian tradition of the 'humanistic revolt of Buddha' (66), a tradition which has surfaced time and again in the various religious (bhakti) and socio-political moves. In a dialogic passage between Conscience and I, Me and Myself, Anand projects his self-questioning of religious Absolutism, of the 'self' as seen as a separation from the Divine. Anand failed to respond to the 'exclusiveness' of Christianity. He writes: 'This exclusiveness is hard for the intelligence to concede in view of the equal heights of moral and spiritual beauty of character achieved by men like the Buddha and Muhammed' (74).[8] Yet was it possible for anyone to be in a permanent state of questioning and disbelief? Anand found 'belief' to be a necessary part of both self-definition and existence, 'I must believe, I must have some touchstone of values to discriminate between the various problems before me. I must have some hypotheses' (79). At some point the self was also part of the world, not only of the Absolute. Anand realised that at some point there needs be a synthesis between the moral and the intellectual. Separation between disciplines, categorisation into narrow frames led to fragmented concepts. It did not give a view of the whole man in any totality (80-81). The best of the liberals believed in trusteeship, in the superiority of the western civilization. Anand lists a few exceptions (85) that favoured freedom. But whether this freedom included the concept of equality remains uncertain specially when we respond to the undercurrents in *A Passage to India* and the ending of the novel (Forster) or *Burmese Days* (Orwell) and Orwell's experience in Marrakech where he felt that the coloured people merged with the earth. They were invisible even in their own environment. Recognition of an injustice and willingness to make the necessary self-erasure need not always go together. Tolerance in its literal meaning does not encompass the sense of 'going across'. The liberal intellectuals recognised the contradiction between imperialism and their notion of freedom but simultaneously they also recognised the invisibility of the oppressed. Their personal need for the freedom of the 'other' was an act of self-preservation while the colonial's need for freedom was an act of survival. The in-between-ness of the European intellectuals, Anand felt, was a betrayal of European culture.[9] For Anand it was necessary to link the purpose and the ethicality to a relationship between means and ends (88). It is in England, in the years during 1926-35, that Anand's humanism, which incorporated both ethicality and resistance, began to take shape. In 1946 when he looks back on this period and the early debates in his mind, he comments upon the Asian intellectuals who had simultaneously encompassed in their consciousness 'both a sense of locality, and a wider, more human outlook' (89).

Throughout the nineteenth century, Indian intelligentsia had grappled with ideas and ideologies from other cultures and political thought was moving towards a greater openness. But somewhere Anand does not take into account the separatists thought that characterised religious reform movements—spurred on perhaps by the divisive policies of the imperial government.[10] The process of intellectual development which Anand describes is also a description of a genuine hybridity of ideas, the catholicity which Gandhi demonstrated in his incorporation of other thinkers, ideologies and religious belief in his ideas and lifestyle all reflect this coming together of cultures. This openness of mind is a necessary constituent of any meaningful humanism. Increasingly, Anand felt inclined towards 'the moral force, which often shamed brute force' (96). The important thing was how one looked at the 'other', whether as a social equal or not; how one looked at his economic and physical needs, his need for space and freedom—in short, how did one proceed to sense the suffering and deprivation of the 'other'. Intellectuals in other times and locations have been faced with this problem, that is the problem of how to get inside the skin of the other, to link with the disinherited. In an interview with Gayatri Spivak, Mahasweta Devi has also talked about this problem. Her personal solution is to go and live with them, 'Tried to solve the problem by seeing everything from his or her point of view' (Mahasweta Devi, v). And she goes on to assert that love and trust alone can be the basis of a relationship (vii). Gandhi's personal solution was to live like the ordinary people and share their deprivation. But these are partial solutions. Amongst others, two constraints which immediately strike one are—first, the inability to off-load one's cultural baggage, intellectual ideas and education, that is, the inability to reduce one's experience and thinking; and second, when one is hungry one cannot think of other things. As Orwell has said when one's stomach is empty, one can only think of an empty stomach. Orwell too went across especially in *Down and Out* in London and Paris. These temporary goings across transform and extend one but the original location in class and mindset would continue to exist as a controlling sensibility.

Anand experienced a sense of guilt for his earlier indifference to social realities—a guilt that we can trace in the works of many an intellectual. Guilt led him to work through self-reflection on an autobiographical novel placed in a socio-political context. Anand writes, 'the theme of my work became the whole man and the whole gamut of human relationships' (118). Anand's sense of intellectual responsibility and his corresponding need for commitment, as one can see, has been a life-long one with ideas and art. It is 'the writer alone, if he is honest and brave', who is in a position 'to understand the world qualitatively, to perceive the most delicate processes of the human sensibility, on the aesthetic as well as the cognitive and conative planes.' Anand goes on to say, 'I want to emphasize the revolutionary aspect of art, I mean the way in which it can change life' (130-31). From guilt to responsibility, from passive or self-centred pursuit of knowledge to the shaping of a vision, from isolation to linking with others, both with other intellectuals and the larger humanity, from belief to a commitment to human relationships—this was the road he travelled. Anand like his contemporaries in India and in England—writers and activists alike—felt that the thirties was a turning point, 'the beginning of a revolutionary era which will either bring to birth, through all screaming and blood, a more egalitarian society based on justice, humanity and a civilized morality or the human race will be wiped out...' (136). None of the two has happened in any fullness—but the intellectual's commitment to humanity is reinforced. It was this sense of commitment that led him to believe in the 'whole man'. He refers to Hind Swaraj on one occasion and to Gandhi on several, to Tagore on a couple of occasions—but is not fully convinced of their practical solutions. In this Anand is mistaken, especially when he labels Gandhi's humanism mystical (141). Gandhi's humanism was an active, this-worldly one as his concern with the socio-political issues shows. Gandhi was concerned both with the dignity of the individual as well as his right to equality. Amulya Ganguli in a recent article on Gandhi writes 'he was not just a freedom fighter like Nelson Mandela. Even as he opposed the British, Gandhi wanted to ensure that Indians were ready for their freedom...' (*The Times of India*, Oct. 4, 2005). Before proceeding on the Dandi March, he wrote in *Young India* on February 27, 1930:

> This time on my arrest, there is to be no mute passive non-violence but non-violence of the most active type should be set in motion so that not a single believer in non-violence as an article of faith for the purpose of achieving India's goal, should find himself free or alive at the end of the effort...whilst, therefore, every effort should be made to restrain the forces of violence, civil disobedience once begun cannot be stopped and must not be stopped so long as there is a single civil resister left free or alive. (Qtd. by Bose, 199)

Anand's use of the word mystical appears to suggest that he, like Orwell, considered a belief in God to be incompatible with humanism, an assumption which cannot be justified on any rational or irrational ground. While religion requires God, ethics does not exclude one. Only the ethical belief does not prioritize God above all things, it does not place God above men but allows him to merge in the conscience. Gandhi had continuously expanded the idea of religion. This takes me back to Anand's dialogue with his own conscience. The conflict is between desire and non-attachment. Anand is questioning religiosity and an obsessive concern with transcendent truths not religion as the source of ethical concerns. Gautama did not accept the dogma of a 'personal God', Gandhi expanded Hindu religion to include other religions, to include the human being. Anand substituted God with ethical commitment while Gandhi expanded religious morality to include righteousness towards others rather than one's own self. His target was the ordinary man whose emotional memory had to be evoked while Anand's target was the intelligentsia. Another difference is that while Gandhi worked through the category of a people and a nation, Anand was using the Marxist ideology of world struggles against capitalism.

Apology for Heroism is not only a statement on humanism—as the term it should be freed from the imperialistic mould—but also a critiquing of the western concepts of Enlightenment and universalism. Buddha's Enlightenment was an intuitive one and not a rational one—based on compassion, not on reason. The values of universalism are also culture based and associated with power. Humanism was perceived not only as the beginning of a new brotherhood where war, violence and hatred could be eliminated but also as a struggle for the new birth of a selfhood, a more worthy selfhood. In a postscript Anand adds that violence may annihilate all else but not the human heart (175). In a still later postscript, Anand goes over the ground once again. The date of the 'Postscript' is not mentioned but in the essay itself Anand writes 'twelve years ago when Apology for Heroism was written' (199) thus placing it in 1957 at the time of the second edition's publication. From 1946 to 1957, a lot has happened: Indian is free, Gandhi is dead, violence and weapons of violence on the increase and Marxism have manifested itself in rigid and still more restrictive forms. There is little to support the belief that human nature will change for the better, or that individual will alone can move the world through ideas. Feeling much less optimistic than he was in 1945, he goes through the history of western philosophy and recalls the Indian philosophical traditions. At this time the reality which stares him in the face is the need for values, values which 'cannot be explained in logical terms', but which include 'certain worlds of inner faculty and experience'. Anand stresses the need for the emotional content of values and writes: 'I realise now that any humanism that is worthwhile must leave room for the world of values which contain elements that transcend the world of facts' (176-77). Later, he also recognises the overlapping between philosophy and religion (180). Analysing his half-acceptance of Marxist ideology, he is aware that his road to socialism had been through Tolstoy, Ruskin, Morris and Gandhi men who vested their faith in an ethical system of values.

Anand is up in arms against the concept of personal salvation, which eliminates the presence of others: salvation needs to be based on shared suffering and shared happiness. Going back to Indian religious thought through Radhakrishnan, Aurobindo or Ramana Maharishi, he is of the view that the alienation of Indian thinkers (from the struggles of others) must end. Gandhi conquered this limitation of religious anchoring and stepped right into life. By now the Absolute is not important but truth is, ideology as an economic reality has been superseded by a concern for the hope, which is now identified not with progress but with the fact of constant struggle: 'the only life is the life of struggle, and that this struggle is continuous and eternal' (202). Political freedom is a means to creative thought and creative participation.

Anand worked his way through philosophy and ideology, through doubt and belief, through a weighing of priorities between the individual and society in order to arrive at a concept of humanism which was an enabling one and was based on the principles of freedom and sharing. Ethics was an integral part of it—code of values not necessarily embedded in any religious base but geared to a connection between emotion and action, a reaching out, a crossing over.

What is casually dismissed as social realism or as Marxist influence in writers like Premchand and Mulk Raj Anand is the coming together of a concern with the disadvantaged other, which is part of the self. Sarat Chandra Chattopadhya who is not referred to by Anand was another older writer (1876-1938), still writing till the thirties whose writing rejected all moral codes and constraints and who looked at the other as a human being—a concern which crossed even gender boundaries. With their idea of social commitment and ethical values, with their belief in humanistic concerns, one can see the 'organic intellectual' at work. Gayatri Spivak refers to Gramsci in her 'Translator's Preface' to the translation of Mahasweta Devi's stories, *Imaginary Maps*. She quotes Gramsci's description: 'Every social group, coming into existence on the original terrain of an essential function in the world of economic production creates together with itself, organically, one or more strata of intellectuals which give it homogeneity and an awareness of its own function not only in the economic but also in the social and political fields' (qtd. by Spivak, xxii). I would like to extend this organicity to a notion of intellectual sharing and responsibility, an evocation of the response of the 'other'. This then is the new humanism which ethical revolution gives birth to, through its ability to dismantle rigid frameworks and models and to step out into the open human terrain, which is in a constant state of flux. This kind of humanism deconstructs the 'self' as well as the 'other' in order to destroy distance and inequality.

NOTES

1. I am using the term 'generation of the thirties' in a very liberal sense and it refers not only to writers born in the first decade of the 20th century but also those writers and political revolutionist who happened to be active at that time even if their revolutions had begun much earlier.
2. The revolutionaries were active both in Punjab and Bengal. Bhagat Singh's Prison Diaries are an evidence of the ethical base of their activities while Gandhi's trial in the Chauri-Chaura case was an example of its own kind. Bose quotes from Gandhi's statement in his book *The Indian Struggle 1920-1942*, when Gandhi had said: 'The only course open to you, the Judge and the Assessors, is either to resign your posts and thus disassociate yourselves from evil if you feel that the law you are called upon to administer is an evil and that in reality I am innocent, or to inflict on me the severest penalty if you believe that the system and the law you are assisting to administer are good for the people of this country and that my activity is therefore injurious to the public weal' (Bose, 83-84).
3. Bose refers to Gandhi as a dictator on more than one occasion in *The Indian Struggle 1920-1942*, though it is besides the point that Bose was fascinated by both Mussolini and Hitler. Also refer chapter XXI of *The Indian Struggle* where Bose's resentment against passive resistance comes to the forc as hc moves away to form the Forward Bloc.
4. "Inside the Whale" critiqued the commitment of the intellectuals of thirties and their communistic leanings. Orwell was critical of left-wing intellectuals as it appeared to him to be a commitment to a narrowing abstract concern which was more ideological than human. This was the period when the nature and need of intellectual commitment was hotly debated. Orwell viewed commitment as being 'true to one's own self' not a party ideology. For more details refer to a talk "Literature and Totalitarianism" broadcast over the BBC in 1941, CEJL II, 134-35. For an interesting commentary see John Rodden's "On the Political Sociology of Intellectuals: George Orwell and the London Left Intelligentsia" in *The Revised Orwell*. Ed. Jonathan Rose, Michigan State University Press, East Langsing, 1992.
5. Nirmal Verma's essay "India and Europe: Some Reflections on the Self and the Other" [Jain, *Creating Theory* (2000) 114].

6. The 'other' has always been there even if it is a spiritual 'other'. True the spiritual 'other' functions as a source of absorption not of separation but nevertheless it is there in a hierarchical relationship.
7. Expatriate experiences have worked differently with different individuals depending on the experience one carries from home, the time of life and purpose for which one travels abroad. The experiences o: Pandita Ramabai—a woman who struggled both against fate and society—and Swami Vivekananda who travelled abroad with a set religious and national purpose must needs be different but the separation which separates one on out account of colour and power is similar. History tells us that revolutionary movements have either been born abroad or have been nurtured there.
8. He goes on to add 'The record of the Christian missionaries in the Colonial and semi-Colonial countries was, except in rare cases like that of C.F. Andrews, not a happy one, in so far as, until very recently, they bore the cross to the far flung places of the earth almost side by side with the Imperial sword' (76).
9. Anand writes: 'But I had found that those very people who were the real custodians of European culture, the intelligentsia, were betraying it, by accepting defeat at the hands of the manoeuvering party politicians and by devoting themselves to their own petty concerns, be these egoistical self-realization, salvation or poetry and art as mere forms of selfish amusement' (187). Aiso refer pp. 80-84.
10. I have in mind those thinkers and events which were based on religious identification and went on to define the nation in terms of religious identities, the division of Bengal in 1905, the exclusion of the tribals from centrality in national life and the separate electorates on religious basis.

REFERENCES

Anand, Mulk Raj. *Apology for Heroism* (1946). New Delhi: Arnold-Heinemann, 1975.

Anand, Mulk Raj. *Untouchable* (1935). New Delhi: Orient Paperbacks, 1970.

Bose, Subhas Chandra. *The Indian Struggle 1920-1942*. Eds. Sisir K. Bose and Sugata Bose (Main manuscript FP 1935 by Lawrence and Wishart). New Delhi: Oxford University Press (1977), 1998.

Devi, Mahasweta. "The Author in Conversation" (with Gayatri Spivak). *Imaginary Maps*. Calcutta: Thema, 1993.

Ganguli, Amulya. "The Mahatma's Case", *The Times of India* (Delhi Edition), October 4, 2005, 16.

Orwell, George. "Inside the Whale", *The Collected Essays, Journalism and Letters of George Orwell*, 4 Vols. (Referred to as CEJL in the text.) Vol. I, Eds. Sonia Orwell and Ian Angus. London: Secker & Warburg, 1968.

Orwell, George. "Literature and Totalitarianism", *The Collected Essays, Journalism and Letters of George Orwell*, 4 Vols. Vol. II, Eds. Sonia Orwell and Ian Angus. London: Secker & Warburg, 1968.

Orwell, George. "Reflections on Gandhi", *The Collected Essays, Journalism and Letters of George Orwell*, 4 Vols. Vol. IV, Eds. Sonia Orwell and Ian Angus. London: Secker & Warburg, 1968.

Rodden, John. "On the Political Sociology of Intellectuals: George Orwell and the London Left Intelligentsia", *The Revised Orwell*. Ed. Jonathan Rose. East Lansing: Michigan University Press, 1992.

Spivak, Gayatri. "Translator's Note", *Imaginary Maps*. Calcutta: Thema, 1993.

Verma, Nirmal. "India and Europe: Some Reflections on the Self and the Other", *Creating Theory: Writers on Writing*. Ed. Jasbir Jain. New Delhi: Pencraft International, 2000.

Anand as a Connoisseur of the Arts

5

A.S. Dasan

I

Remembering Mulk Raj Anand is to foreground the aesthetics of compassionate humanism as the highest pursuit in life. Anand, as novelist and art-critic, was a discerning and trend-setting contributor to the heritage of humanism which has its deep roots in Indian culture and aesthetics. His knowledge of both the devotional and the secular traditions of Indian aesthetics, Indian thought and visual arts, and his ceaseless pursuit of truth as the finest signifier of the fullness of man, rested on and revolved around his love for humanity, particularly his option for the poor and the oppressed. The swan song of Anand was that 'I am a humanist and I wish all that's humane prevail on earth'. This was part of the last poetic statement Anand made in an interview this writer had with him about three months before his passage into eternity.

To many of us who knew him closely, Anand was a 'Renaissance man' with an open mind towards the outbursts of mental energy. As a Renaissance man, he strived to promote the spirit of modernism that signified the concerns of living with dignity in the present, celebrate new forms of humanism, and build connections towards harmony blending the intellectual and the emotional in the midst of existential angst. His sense of 'shaping the Indian modern' was in tune with the learning he did in Europe and with the aspirations of many other thinkers of his time in India. His worldview exuded a sense of contemporaneity and hovered around a ceaseless search for truth and freedom. Branding him as a writer with leftist leanings or stereotyped didacticism would be a one-eyed view.

As a connoisseur of life, he believed in 'the freedom of the mind and the senses as the source of thoughts and forms'. He was never satisfied with a repetitive existence, an existence that blocks critical enquiry and creative alternatives for a richer civilization. His artistic tastes evolved and grew out of his secular impulses. The cause of human dignity and universal freedom inspired him throughout his writing career. "Freedom", as Suresh Kohli put it in his tribute on the eve of Anand's 99th birthday, was "the protagonist of almost all his fictional works" (*The Hindu*, 2003).

As writer and art-critic, he was a rebel within, a pilgrim with a heart of dissent, searching for truth, truth that would reveal the whole man and usher in understanding and comradeship against pain and brutality of existence. His early novels, particularly *Untouchable* (1934) and *Coolie* (1935)—two world classics in terms of sense of form and purpose—reveal his awareness of the true measure of the damage oppression of different sorts could cause. His later novels, particularly *Nine Moods of Bharata* (1999) and *Of Power and Pity* (2000) reflect his mellowed moods, moving beyond ire and indignation and tending a pilgrimage towards transcendent possibilities. His setting of Indian sculpture, artistic monuments and cave paintings depicting tales of compassion serves as the pilgrimage motif for transcendence in these two later novels. Existential humanism, with hope in the morrow, was a supreme mover of his sociological imagination and art-criticism as well. The Indian perception of the **'third Eye'**, the eye of discernment, and the aesthetic experience of *karuna rasa* unified his social and artistic sensibilities. His immense contribution to the cause of art-criticism may be better understood in the light of this introductory reflection.

II

A versatile genius and master of varied *genres* who was particular to fuse the functional integrity of art with life, Anand was also a cultural critic and connoisseur of the arts. His commitment to and involvement in art appreciation became a kind of passion, passion to communicate 'felt-experiences' of his perception and understanding of the cultural and artistic history of India and other countries as well. All the arts, in his view, were to serve as means of diffusing and keeping alive the heritage of compassionate humanism. Anand's affinity with this heritage has its roots in his artisan family background and his interest in the visual and plastic arts since his childhood days. In her book, *The Wisdom of the Heart: A Study of the Works of Mulk Raj Anand* (1985), Marlene Fisher narrates how Anand's uncles were instrumental in 'opening his eyes' to the gentle and picturesque Kangra valley of the lower Himalayas, to the religious and philosophical significance of Pahari (literally meaning mountain) paintings done in Basholi style and exquisite miniature forms, and to the Graeco-Roman-Indian basis of the Gandharan art which was the first in history to portray the Lord Buddha in human form and produced the best pieces of sculpture and monuments to commemorate the Jataka tales of compassion and wisdom.

Anand's stay in London for more than twenty years turned out to be a gateway that opened his eyes to a galaxy of thought and a holistic worldview. Anand arrived in London in 1924. It was a journey in search of higher pursuits in life, beyond 'id, ego and super ego'. It was a journey that helped him shape his critical thinking and cultivate a worldview rooted in Indianness, Indianness known for accommodating, celebrating and enriching the spirit of eclecticism. Well known dancer and cultural czarina, Kapila Vatsyayan's recording of the conversation of Anand with her in 1999 when he was 95—which runs into three parts under the title, 'Living Legends', is an important source of information besides Anand's *Apology for Heroism* (1946) and *Conversations in Bloomsbury* (1981) to follow up the progression of his career as a writer and connoisseur of the arts as well. His mental war with ideas had a passage through 'the literary intermodernism of London', to use a phrase of Kristin Bluemel, which played a major role in shaping his aesthetic sensibilities. Since the time he joined the University of London for higher studies, Anand's approach to realities was destined to be philosophical. As Jag Mohan remarks, Anand "came under the benign influence of Prof. G. Dawes Hicks who guided him in his doctoral thesis on John Locke, George Berkeley and David Hume" (84). His befriending a considerable number of radical thinkers and modernist writers of literary London helped him enlarge and enrich his freedom of thought and expression, his view of the dignity of the human person and his dissent against Fascist tendencies.

A chance meeting with Ananda Coomaraswamy made a big impact upon his outlook on Indian culture. Coomaraswamy's orthodox interpretation of the Hindu view of art, namely 'beauty is perfection or God' and 'creative art is a mental activity inspired and impacted by some spiritual force working within the artist', appealed to him although he was inclined towards propounding 'a humanist aesthetic'. Under the impact of Coomaraswamy, whom he considered as his great teacher, Anand was able to see the damage the British colonizers had done to the Indian psyche, Indian culture and Indian aesthetic sensibilities. His interaction with Eric Gill enabled him to be an active member of Modern Architects Researchers' Society (MARS) in London. Soon after the completion of his doctoral studies, he concentrated on his writing career which simultaneously evolved in twofold directions, namely sociological imagination through fiction and art-criticism through evaluation of different visual arts. The common ingredient in both the directions was his major preoccupation with cultural, literary and artistic aesthetics and his compassionate worldview.

Other impacts such as his visit to the treasures of the Louvre Museum in Paris in the company of Irene Rhys, his Irish girl-friend, his periodic visits to the British Museum in London, his listening to André Malraux's (1901-76) articulation of the 'Voices of Silence' in art objects, his interaction with Bloomsbury literary group, his familiarity with Clive Bell's (1881-1964) aesthetic concept of 'significant forms' in art, and his grasp of 'Modernism' in art through his acquaintance with Roger Fry (1866-1934) and Herbert Read (1893-1968), two well-known art-critics of the early twentieth century who were also associated with the British National Gallery and with *The Burlington Magazine*, devoted to the fine and decorative arts, published since 1903 and continued even today without a break, had their profound impact in his interpretations of various art-forms. His readings of William Morris and John Ruskin had an impact upon his effort to combine political consciousness and aesthetic sensibilities and integrate them within the hermeneutics of the arts.

Eric Gill (1882-1940), a well-known master craftsman, engraver and typographer who defined art as 'a skilful activity in a state of freedom', drew Anand's attention to the significance of the religious and the erotic dimensions of engravings and inspired him to see in better light similar or related Indian artefacts. It was Eric Gill who did an engraving to Anand's short story, "The Lost Child" (1929) which was included in *Great Short-stories of the World* (1934) published by Odhams, London. As mentioned earlier, Ananda K. Coomaraswamy (1877-1947), the then curator of Indian and Islamic arts at the Boston Museum of Fine Arts, author of *The Dance of Shiva: Essays on Indian Art and Culture* (1918) and pioneer in promoting non-European art-criticism, was another great influence in the mind of Anand. Coomaraswamy was aware of the biased, prejudiced and narrow understanding of Indian art, philosophy, architecture and culture by the West. He critiqued 'the holier than thou' attitude of the West vis-à-vis Indian art and expressed his dissent against the European agenda of 'measuring other civilizations by the degree to which they approximate to Western civilization'. He saw and understood how and how much Indian art suffered during the British colonial era in India. Against the backdrop of European imperialism, Coomaraswamy tried to inspire a new life to understand and conserve different categories of Indian civilization—architecture, music, handicrafts, popular and classic literature and schools of philosophy. His analytical mind that had the capacity to appreciate multidimensional universalism rather than mere essentialism was appealing to Anand.

III

In 1930 when he was just 25, Anand made his debut as an art-critic by writing a slim volume of forty pages on 'Persian Painting' (1930), and two years later, under the guidance of

Coomaraswamy, his monograph on 'The Hindu View of Art' (1932), mirroring the integration of religion and philosophy as the basis of the Hindu view of art and life and the experience of wholeness as the essence of classical Indian art, was published. In his Preface to the first edition of 'The Hindu View of Art', Anand states:

> There has so far been no book on the Hindu view of art responding to the available introductions to various European system of aesthetics. Mr. Havell's *Ideals of Indian Art* was more concerned to explain particular examples of Indian art in the light of the Hindu view of art than with that view as such, and all that is available on the topic are Dr. Coomoaraswamy's two small essays included in his admirable *Dance of Shiva*. In the following essay I have attempted to elaborate the plan laid out by Dr. Coomaraswamy, and have sought to supply such a short, simple expression of the Hindu view of art as might interest the average uninitiated reader (14).

In the Prefaces to the second (1956) and third (1987) editions of the monograph, he notes how this monograph, the first flush of his youthful endeavour, has witnessed to the stages of maturity in his thinking vis-à-vis 'the conflicts between the demands of tradition and the compulsions of modernity'. The inclusion of an introductory essay on 'Art and Reality' by Eric Gill in the first edition of the monograph, and the essays, 'The Philosophy of Ancient Asiatic Art' by Ananda Coomaraswamy, 'A Bird's Eye View of Indian Aesthetic' by K.C. Pandey, and 'The Symbolic Aspects of Form' by Alice Boner, in the subsequent editions of the monograph indicates Anand's genuine and humble acknowledgement of the limitations of his own perception of the heritage of Indian art and aesthetics and his capacity for accommodating eclectic views on art, form and reality as well.

Anand's return to India, prompted by his inner urge to celebrate freedom and beckoned by his love for India with all her strengths and weaknesses, may be seen as a major event that shaped the next forty years of his life as a pilgrimage to various heritage sites of India. Anand had a crystal clear idea of the history of medieval India vis-à-vis emperor Akbar's artistic pursuits and his patronage to multifarious artistic activities. Realizing how 'a mere religious inspiration' or absolutist view of art 'could be no guarantee of deeply felt expression in a time when the Post-Renaissance ideas and 'form of the West' had become part of Indian culture, Anand was more and more inclined to include and celebrate 'all that exalts man, uplifts him, and inspires him to higher consciousness or intense awareness of the cosmos, in the past or present', within the scope of his vision of aesthetics.

The launching of *Marg*, the journal of arts, meaning 'pathway', in 1946, a culturally significant milestone in the post-independent India, in collaboration with the Tata Group, courtesy Dr. Homi Babha, the atomic physicist and an artist of merit, was a concrete manifestation of Anand's commitment not only to "rediscover the heritage of Indian and Asian art through the centuries" and to examine "the contemporary trends in architecture, sculpture, painting and graphic design" but also to his plural, integral and holistic hypothesis of a humanist and compassionate worldview. The incredibly rich cultural heritage of India, and the damage the British colonialism had done to the Indian mind vis-à-vis appreciation of India's cultural heritage, prompted him to found *Marg*. The graceful gesture of the House of Tata to support Anand's aims and goals through *Marg* was part of the grand vision and aspiration of the Tata group to build a new India.

The successful launch of the Progressive Artists' Group in 1948, popularly known as PAG, preceded by the unexpected arrival of European painters/sculptors like Langhammer, E. Schlesinger and Rudi von Leyden in India because they wanted to escape Hitler's Nazism, was an important event that ushered in the contemporary art movement in India. This was the time when Indian art movement moved beyond the contours of single or monarchic support and began to blossom forth with more and more individuals and groups coming forward with fresh ideas for art display, practices and promotions. As a quiet revolution was taking place with happenings of art events, exchange of ideas and establishment of private art galleries in places like Baroda, Bombay, Delhi and Calcutta, the Indian government set up the Indian Council for Cultural Relations 'for cultural exchanges with the rest of the world' (indianartcircle.com) in 1950, the National Gallery of Modern Art in Delhi in 1954, with enough space for exhibitions, and the Lalith Kala Akademi in the same year. The contemporary movement, pioneered by Paris trained Amrita Shergil, N.S. Bendre, K.K. Hebbar, Binod Bihari Mukherjee, Nirode Mazumdar and others, was strengthened later by M.F. Hussein, F.N. Souza, Akbar Padamsee, Gaitonde, Krishan Khanna, Jehangir Sabavala, Swaminathan, Satish Gujral, Bhupen Khakkhar, Tyeb Mehta, Vivan Sundaram and several others. As India's foremost and astute art-critic, Anand was the first to speak and write about modernism in Indian art by spotting the talent, individual styles, professionalism and dedication of India's progressive artists like M.F. Hussein, S.H. Raza and F.N. Souza.

To Anand, via *Marg*, tradition meant "innovation of the past, part of the human metabolism, the warp and woof of our inheritance, in which we are clothed. We take these innovations for granted" (qtd. in Mursi Saad El-Din's write-up on Anand in *AL-AHRAM* [Cairo] 21-27 October 2004). Anand's effort through *Marg* was to liberate Indian minds from debilitating complexes vis-à-vis the art scene of India. It was in view of this effort that he tried to make India's mythic and artistic past relevant to our times. The aesthetics he put in and the explorative content he integrated within select superb and beautiful visual arts depicting the depths of varied forms of Indian art inspired Jawahar Lal Nehru, then Prime Minister of India, to suggest that the State should buy a thousand copies of every issue of *Marg* for distribution. Although Anand was aware of the poverty of response in India, he felt an urge to move forward with hope in action. The encouraging response from abroad was another propeller that made him move forward. Today, by virtue of the foundational wisdom Anand had put in, *Marg* has embraced a broad cultural and historical view of the arts accommodating varied perspectives and providing space for multiple interpretations.

Anand's active involvement with the edition of *Marg* for more than three decades may be viewed as the most significant manifestation of his convictions about the utility of the arts. His vast knowledge of tradition as a shared value, his familiarity with modernity of thought, his philosophical approach to realities, and his poetic vision of life and his spirit of eclecticism enabled him to befriend distinguished minds like Hermann Goetz, W. Archer and Karl Khandelwalla and seek their guidance for the edition of *Marg*. Every issue of *Marg* he edited turned out to be a breviary of synthesis of Indian arts. In his tribute to Goetz, Anand noted how Goetz was a great admirer of Indian art and symbolic meanings of Indian sculptures and myths. In his essay, *The Third Eye*, he records his appreciation for Jamini Roy for his artistic affinities with the soil, the earth colours and the folk culture of peasant genius. His grasp of the paintings of Amrita Shergil made him realize that Indian sculptures and paintings contained infinite space for symbolic connotations and meanings. Anand's perception of Indian arts, as he articulates in his Editorial of the 100th issue of *Marg*, conveys that there is something deeper and more than what meets the eye in the arts. The arts instill a 'divine discontent'—a longing for communion between the physical and the social, and the mundane and the cosmic. Creativity manifests a sense of synergic worldview.

IV

In his effort to popularize art—appreciation in India, Anand was so passionate that little of the spectrum of Indian arts escaped his attention. His musings on 'The Indian Theatre' (1950) are a panoramic survey of the diversity and the ethos of Indian theatres. His understanding of the journey of Indian painting was insightful, comprehensive and holistic. He surveyed it from the classical Ajanta to the modern via the period of oblivion during the British rule. His writings—his own and those written in collaboration with others—on topics such as 'The Bride's Book of Beauty' (1947), reissued as 'The Book of Indian Beauty' (1981), 'Homage to Khajuraho' (1960), which has the largest group of medieval Hindu temples, famous for their erotic sculpture with nothing left to imagination, 'Konark'

(1968), the site of the 13th century Sun temple of the Ganga dynasty, 'Indian Ivories' (1970), 'Ajanta' (1971), and Ellora, celebrated for their rock-cut cave art and architectures, and 'Album of Indian Paintings' (1973), are reflections of timeless significance. If some of these sites are part of World Heritage sites today, the credit goes to Anand also for his multidimensional way of appreciating art. His seminal essay, 'Is there a Contemporary Civilization?' (1963), read along with his lecture on 'The Third Eye: A Lecture on the Appreciation of Art' (1963), delivered as the first Tagore Professor of art at Panjab University, Chandigarh, courtesy A.C. Joshi, illustrious Vice-Chancellor of the University then, who had an eye for talent, and his imaginative and educative monograph on 'Seven Little-Known Birds of the Inner Eye' (1978) may be cited here as primary source books to understand and appreciate the holistic mind of Anand vis-à-vis his commitment and dedication to art appreciation. His editions on 'Ananda Kentish Coomaraswamy' (1956), 'Contemporary World Sculpture' (1968), 'Homage to Jaipur' (1977), 'Homage to Amritsar' (1977), 'Homage to Kalamkari' (1979), 'Splendours of Kerala' (1980), 'Golden Goa' (1980), 'Splendours of the Vijayanagara' (1980), and 'Splendours of Himachal Heritage' (1997) are a treat to the mind of the reader. Most of these editions are part of the *Marg* treasure. If *Marg* could look for select ones of Anand's writings on the arts and publish them in different volumes, it will be a service to the present day reader. It would be one way of keeping alive the heritage of Anand's effort to popularize the Indian arts.

Urban planning and modern architecture were part of Anand's artistic concerns. If only the vision of greater Bombay, envisaged in collaboration with other visionaries, architects and designers like Charles Correa and his associates at the initiative of Anand, and textured with visuals in *Marg* issues, had been implemented without dilution, Bombay would not have been a city of such a strange symbiosis as it is seen today. Their visions and plans were hallmarks of social responsibility. Improving the quality of life, beyond the scope of beautification of parks and monuments and regulating the ever increasing and never ending traffic jams, was uppermost in their minds. As Shekhar Krishnan comments in his writings on "Mumbai Vision 2010" (shekhar@crit.org.in), one could have only nostalgic feelings when one compares Anand's and Correa's visionary dreams with 'the Mckinsey type of urban—brand buildings' the present-day architects and image-makers tend to design in their attempt to turn Mumbai into Shanghai or Singapore or London or New York. Money-spinning marketing of architecture and urban designs could mean, if not already, dearth of quality of life and inevitable decay and death of the city.

The Bride's Book of Beauty, co-authored by Anand and Krishna Nehru Hutheesing, serves like an anthological manual on feminine sensibilities, formulas of female beauty, and female social experience. Critics like Kristin Bluemel view the feminist content of the book as the manifestation of Anand's affinities with 'Marxist utopian' notions of 'egalitarian civilization' and women's empowerment. Political discussions apart, the authors' perception of Indian female beauty in the book is adorned with a fine blend of poetry and prose, proverbs and aphorisms, folktales and myths, history and trans-history, anthropology and culture studies, and romance and aesthetics. An Indian bride complete with her *solah shringar* (sixteen adornments) from head to toe is, as the authors compliment, 'a vision of beauty' that reflects not only 'the traditions of the past' but also her own sense of 'self-consciousness accentuated by her desire to shine'. The wedding day is the most important day in her life and all the adornments symbolize the significance of the day. The day signifies her coy movement into the household of her husband. It is also the day when she realizes that there is a shift from focusing on the aesthetic to the pragmatic sides of life, and hence the special significance of her adornments for the day.

Anand's grasp of *Bharata Natyam* echoes, as Pamyla A. Stiehl observes, "Universal and inclusive sentiments" (http://www.rtjournal.org/vol_3/no_2/stiehl.html). Anand contends that *Bharata Natyam* incites "intense awareness in those who can read behind the symbols of any faith the meaning of their own individual spiritual struggles" (6). Like the practitioners and choreographers of the dance, he too was aware of the spiritual component and power of *Bharata Natyam* suggesting an obliteration of the ego which facilitates a synthesis of a higher order connoting spiritual transcendence and wholeness. And such centredness on wholeness is a way of participating in the essence of divinity.

Anand paid rich tributes to the pioneering initiatives taken by the Tagore family in the Revivalist movement that ushered in the Bengal School of Arts and Paintings. His writings on Rabindranath Tagore's vision of humanism and his approach to painting, particularly Tagore's ability to use 'his pen as brush and turn his words into pictures' in a rhythmic and surrealistic manner in his effort to articulate 'imperceptible feelings' echoing 'the collective unconscious of his time'. His monograph titled, *Poet-Painter: Paintings by Rabindrnath Tagore* (1985) is an enlightening study and personal homage to Tagore's creative genius and his heritage of multidimensional Renaissance—wisdom, a scintillating synthesis of traditional aesthetics, humanistic spirituality, mysticism and early modernism.

As an art-critic who had already travelled all over the world and seen the best of the arts, Anand was astounded by the uniqueness of the caves of Ajanta. With reference to the caves of Ajanta, he averred that 'here was something made in 2nd century B.C.' whereas 'the best of the arts of the West were all 15-17th century A.D.'. Marveling at the extraordinary achievements of "our people" from 2nd century B.C. onward, he commented that the stone panel in Mahabalipuram could pale everything else into insignificance. The *Marg* issues, edited by him—136 issues—may be viewed as one single multifaceted album containing a time span from centuries prior to the Christian Era to the modern times offering a spectacular visual feast to the eyes of the beholder and providing plenty of insightful interpretations and comparative analyses as food for thought for both general and specialized studies of Indian art. His sense of the glorious past of the classical traditions of Indian art did not restrict or constrain him from appreciating the relevance or the stylistic variations in modern art. His eclectic mind was receptive to new beauteous forms transfiguring realities and ushering in moods of contemplation through creative innovations. The first triennial showcasing global contemporary art in India in 1968, an event that attracted the best from different parts of the world, was the brainchild of Anand whose contacts with the art and the literary fraternity of the world went back to his participation in the International Brigade in Spain for the cause of human freedom.

Holding on to his grasp of the arts as mirrors reflecting the cultural and aesthetic sensibilities of civilizations, he wrote path-breaking essays and articles with clinical precision on varied phases of the heritage of the arts of Indian civilization—from the Ancient to the Medieval, from the Medieval to the Contemporary and from the Contemporary to the Modern. With illustrations of visuals and in the light of his pilgrimage-visits and journeys to places of historical importance and artefacts of enduring significance, accompanied by Dolly Sahiar, one of his soul-mates for a long time until her demise in May 2004, followed by his own in September 2004, Anand portrayed the arts as an indicator of the broader developments in society and the new directions towards which it was likely to proceed in terms of achievements and failures and hopes and impediments. In the process, he also discerned the changes and shifts within the world of the arts due to the impact of cross-cultural and cross-media influences.

As a beholder of the beauty behind the arts, music, dance, paintings, sculptures, architectures, frescos and such other visuals, Anand never subscribed to the French or Oscar Wildean perception of 'all arts as useless'. He critiqued 'the machine civilization' for its failure to appreciate the utility of all the arts and for its incapacity to 'produce human beings with a total awareness'. Anand subscribed to the aphorism of Ananda Coomaraswamy that 'everyman is an artist but an artist is a special kind man'.

In a signed but undated essay on "Appreciation of Art", which has been slated to be part of *Anand's Prose Anthology—Select Essays*, being edited by Nalini Dasan and this writer, Anand states why he looks up to the primitive man—his sense of precision in sharpening his arrow, as a referential to speak of the instinctive love in man to look "for perfection, for coherence, for making things really well when he is doing a job of work, for relating himself to the indefinable source of creation, for getting into the centre of gravity inside himself and for discovering the unknown outside him in the light of his own awareness". He reiterates the same idea in the following words:

> Again, you give a child some charcoal and the little one will begin to draw on the floor. If you are so generous as to favour it with some coloured crayons and paper, inevitably, in a hundred percent of these cases, the infant will come back with a painting. And if you keep these paintings of the child from the age of three onward till the age of nine or eleven, you will notice that, without any teaching, the child will freely go into those years of growth from the scribble to the doodle, to forms and colours (red for father's face and green for mother's), and end beyond the one dimensional, two dimensional worlds of the primitive, the three dimensional accuracies and ultimately in many dimensions of growing consciousness....
>
> There is, then clearly, a kinetic rhythm in the human body-soul, which will always express itself. Even those who find art useless, and say they don't need it, have this compulsive instinct in them.... This love of perfection is a basic human trait in all ages.

Anand himself was an amateur painter. As a cultural aesthete and humanist to the core who believed in the power of the arts to transform human lives, Anand believed in the utility of all the arts. He viewed the arts as 'a necessity rather than a luxury' as long as they reflected society. He cautioned that no art could stand aloof. He saw Puritanical approach to art as a tendency to indulge in 'soulless formalism', which in turn 'allies itself with nihilism'. Soulless formalism, as all those who vouch for humanism understand, causes decay of sensibility and leads to despair. The Indian heritage of rootedness in compassionate humanism vis-à-vis the arts implies that 'life asserts itself', as Anand states, and seeks inspiration for vitality through poetic celebration and idealization of our cultural sensibilities. K.D. Verma's two chapters on Anand in his book, *The Indian*

Imagination—Critical Essays on Indian Writing in English (2000) is an illuminating study in this direction. While chairing a session on "The 'Other' and Mother India: Art, Poetry and Cultural Criticism" in a Conference (2005) organized by USACLALS Chapter, K.D. Verma also reiterated Anand's contribution as a critic of the arts to the renaissance of cultural sensibilities with reference to the intersections of Indian and Western aesthetics.

In Indian art and aesthetics, sculpting or depicting the romantic heroine is an occasion to celebrate love with its varied dimensions. Despite a minor setback in his later years when he was charged with plagiarism vis-à-vis his write up to *Ever Green Review* of New York on the Indian erotica, Anand held on to his views and continued to write on the artistic and the human significance of the erotica. To Anand, nudity or the rhythms of the erotic in art were not an obscene thing. He emphasized on the role of the erotic art in the development of the individual self. He did not subscribe to Victorian prudery or brahminical piety. He critiqued the idea of restricting discussions on the beauty of the body or the experience of sexual union to 'furtive corners'. His affinities with Gandhian or Leftist contemporaries did not prevent him from appreciating the role of the erotic art in human life. He wanted Indians to come out of 'buttoned—up feelings', gear desire beyond the impact of sex and lust, and elevate it as an enduring moment of celebration of love. He had the wisdom to articulate, without misrepresentation, the tenderness behind coital practice.

In *Kama Kala: Some Notes on the Philosophical Basis of Hindu Erotic Sculpture* (1958), Anand states: "There is a mutual enjoyment which excites not laughter but reverence.... Worship of the sun [was] demonstrated in the energy which brings the human couples together.... The male and female forms thus become the manifestation of duality desired by the Supreme God, the earthly symbols of manliness and procreation. And just as our human love is seen as a symbol of the great love of the Supreme God, so the Joy of physical union reflects the limitless Joy of the Deity in creation" (32).

At the dawn of civilization, nudity in the arts was part of India's social and cultural life. It was never seen to be a vulgar exposure. As part of artistic creation and artistic visuals kept in prominent public places, nudity in the arts was projected as a celebration, as a thing of joy instilling a sense of reverence in the mind of the onlooker. As Aileen Goodson observes in his book, *Therapy, Nudity and Joy*, even the Greeks—the gymnosophists and others—were inspired by nude ascetics in India—the *Ajivikas* and disciples of such other sects who were content with 'being clothed with the sky' as a path towards 'spiritual discipline' that ensured and enhanced 'self-assurance and independent thought'. Today, Jain *munis* continue this tradition as a sign of total renunciation.

V

Today, we are in postmodern times. Less said the better about the nudity shown in the media. Someone pays the media to show and there are people ready and willing to view with little concern for morality or aesthetics. Western influx and media presentation of the physical body, particularly the female body, have corrupted the concept of beauty in nudity and altered the aesthetic sensibilities of the beholder. Postmodern versions of nudity have little to with the development of the individual self or the cultivation of cultural or aesthetic sensibilities. Today, marketing nudity is a money-spinning activity. If nudity is no more an object of reverence, the mindset of the postmodern man, influenced by the media, is to blame. As Meenakshi Thapan of the Department of Sociology, Delhi University, remarks, 'nudity is in vogue in India for all wrong reasons'. Moral policing is detested. If one exposes with 'bare-dare' outfits, he/she is considered liberal and objections are overruled.

Anand's experiences as Tagore Professor of Literature and Fine Arts at the Panjab University in the 1960s and as Fellow of all the three National Akademies, Lalit Kala Akademi, Sangeet Natak Akademi and Sahitya Akademi—a unique honour and record even today—converged in the birth of 'Lokayata' (1970), meaning, 'people's way'. As Founder of Lokayata, Anand tried to use the Centre initially for 'an experiment in community living' with an option for the poor within the ambience of Hauz Khas village in New Delhi via the process of social awareness education and promotion of creative indigenous arts. As a humanist—artist and art-critic, he was also particular to promote through Lokayata those arts which would focus on and manifest the hidden beauty and wisdom of the struggle of the people living on the edge of society. It was also his objective to inspire, prepare and equip young men and women passing through Lokayata to face the challenges of 21st century so as to usher in a world of peace wherein a compassionate view of life, integral humanism and humane solidarity could reign and prevail.

Since recent years, Lokayata has been concentrating on art-exhibition programmes. Periodic exhibitions of creative arts by known, unknown, young and budding artists have been a major activity attracting hundreds of visitors and art-lovers from far and wide. Various themes, focusing on different faith dimensions, Hindu mythology in calendar art, folk and tribal art, heritage continuum highlighting the rich Indian culture, implications of communalism, farmers' resilience on canvas, personal and social impact of poverty, and nature as inspiration have been featured. Landscape, scenic beauty, rural and coastal life, particularly the Konkan region of Maharashtra, have been showcased in some of the works displayed. Art history is one such theme, which the Bengal School of Art represented in its Exhibits by the younger generation. Motifs and colours used by the Gond and the Bhil tribes of Madhya Pradesh and Chattisgarh in painting their walls have been recaptured and exhibited by young artists by way of addressing contemporary social issues. Exhibition of paintings by Tihar inmates, inaugurated in Oct.-Nov. 2004, went on for more than month. Mr. V.P. Singh, Former Primer Minister of India, inaugurated an exhibit of water—colour drawings and paintings by Das Mohan Singh in Nov. 2004. The spirit of Mulk has been the inspiration and propeller behind all these exhibition programmes and activities. It is only natural and befitting that this Centre, after the demise of Anand, is known as 'Lokayata—Mulk Raj Anand Cente'. On the occasion of Anand's birth centenary celebrations organized by Lokayata from 11th to 13th Dec. 2004 and inaugurated by Dr. Manmohan Singh, three significant events were part of the celebrations. One was the launch of the Penguin edition of *The Mulk Raj Anand Omnibus* (2004), edited by Saros Cowasjee, another was the First Anand Memorial Lecture delivered by this writer at India International Centre (IIC), New Delhi, and the other was the exhibition of one hundred one paintings—done as a colourful tribute to Anand—by known and lesser-known artists of different hues, shades and calibre.

VI

To conclude, Anand as the connoisseur of the arts was more than a popularizer of art-appreciation. His contribution to art-criticism was another way of articulating his commitment to compassionate humanism and holistic way of understanding and living, cultivating and nurturing affinities with all that is humane. He was of the view that the arts had the capacity to soothe the mind and sensitize the beholder to empathize with 'understanding culture' rather than 'cognition culture'. Cognition culture reduces everything into an epistemological abstraction whereas understanding culture assimilates and embraces a holistic and compassionate worldview. Rooted in the Indic tradition of *karuna—rasa*, Anand was a Renaissance—man and cultural historicist as well who tried to redefine the canons of art-appreciation via integral humanism in the context of transition from tradition to modernism. That he was 'a leftist to the boot' or 'an atheist in his approach to truth' could be refuted on the grounds of his capacity to appreciate Indian art in its variegated beauty and form—both the devotional and the secular. His sense of the divine and his approach to truthfulness in art enriched his vision of integral humanism despite odds. It was his holistic grasp of life and art that sustained his inner calm in his advanced age and in the evening of his life within the ambience of Khandala where he decided to spend the rest of his life—his late nineties—in the company of the poor. The interiors of the dilapidated cottage in which he spent the last phase of his life were painted with his own favourite colours—yellow and orange-red. One or two antiques from the world of sculpture and one or two paintings—both folklore and modern—filled symbolically the empty space of the walls of the cottage signifying his love and passion for the visuals of the world of arts.

His last phase novels such as *Nine Moods of Bharata* (1998), and *Power and Pity* (2001) hovering around a kind of autobiographical historiography communicate a quest for a pilgrimage towards a holistic understanding of life via reflections on the art-heritage of India. As art-critic, Anand was convinced that art, at its greatest, could liberate the spirit. From this angle, Kavitha Singh's article, "Mulk Raj Anand: A Visionary Aesthete" in *Reflections on the Arts in India* (2000), edited by Pratapaditya Pal and *Marg*'s publication of a special number, titled, *Mulk Raj Anand—Shaping the Indian Modern* (2005), edited by Annapurna Garimella, may be read as fine tributes to Anand's heritage of art-criticism.

One wonders, when we think of the present-day 'don't-care or peripheral attitudes' towards our cultural heritage, whether it is a sign of the neglect of our own cultural heritage. Are our aspirations and dreams to sustain continuity of values so stillborn that we can only sulk and grumble? Prem Shankar Jha's thought-provoking write up, titled "The Infant We killed", in memory of Anand, in *Outlook India*, dated 11th October 2004, points out why Anand could be seen as "one among the idealists defeated by an India gone ape". The author of the article asks:

> Why are architects like Charles Correa, Raj Rival and Satish Grover, who have studied Indian architectural forms exhaustively and sought to incorporate some of their basic elements into their work, now doing most of their work abroad? Why unlike every metropolitan nation does India not have a classical music channel on FM radio anywhere in the country? .... Why, in the bookshops of Mumbai, Delhi or Bangalore has Marg been submerged under an avalanche of new magazines that 'sell' Bollywood and beauty contests as Indian culture?

The sense of loss communicated in the write up is understandable. Yet, the spirit of Anand should prevail. Anand, despite hurdles and difficulties, strongly believed in moving ahead with a profound sense of optimism. Money laundering or Mammonization of the arts never disturbed him to the extent that he would give up looking for or appreciating whatever was beautiful and illumining. He never subscribed to the kind of elitism or elite-centrism that was inclined to distance from the plight of the poor or to remain cynical or sulking. Via art-criticism, he was perpetually committed to liberate humanity crushed by exploitation. He had an indomitable spirit for freedom. India free from all forms of oppression was part of his enlightened and integral vision of humanism. A man of his calibre and equanimity could seldom feel defeated. True, he too rued over falling standards, loss of values, indignities heaped upon the poor, human depravity, moral degradation and the lack of urgency in recognizing the rights of the deprived but he never slipped into a state of helplessness and despair. He believed in action as a reason for hope. A confidence in the morrow moved him to write and poetically indicate the yonder, the infinite possibilities of transfiguration and transcendence.

In 2001, when *The Sunday Tribune* chose to commemorate the bicentennial year of the coronation of Maharaja Ranjit Singh by inviting eminent writers to comment, Anand wrote a feature article on his patronage to the promotion of the arts which was, in fact, an excerpt from his original piece that appeared in one of the issues of *Marg*, and in which he observed in retrospection:

> Our recalls of the heritages of the past are not from the wish to revive bygone splendours, which cannot come back. We wish to show how the purposive will of men in certain periods of our history has created, out of anarchy and disorder, glories which heightened the quality of life and which may inspire our renascent efforts today (http://allaboutsikhs.com/ranjit/ranjit14.htm).

As a writer has already complimented, it would not be an overstatement if this tribute to 'the truthfulness of Maharaja Ranjit Singh' as the patron of the arts were to be extended also as a tribute to Anand's own contribution to the heritage of humanism via his art-criticism.

REFERENCES

Anand, Mulk Raj. *The Hindu View of Art* (1932). New Delhi: Arnold-Heinemann, Third Edition, 1987.

——. "Bharata Natyam: Indian Classical Dance Art" in *Bharata Natyam.* Edited by Sunil Kothari. Bombay: Marg Publications, 1979.

——. *Kama Kala: Some Notes on the Philosophical Basis of Hindu Erotic Sculpture*, London: Skilton, 1958.

Kohli, Suresh. "Sheer Glory". *The Hindu*—Online Edition, Dec. 11, 2003.

Mohan, Jag. "Mulk Raj Anand's Marg: A History and Perspective". *South Asian Review*, Vol. XV, No. 12, July 1991, 83-89.

6

Writing as Activism: Mulk Raj Anand's Commitment to His Ideology

Tutun Mukherjee

The powerful movements that swept through the world during the first few decades of the twentieth century could hardly leave an intellectual unaffected. Such was their impact upon the young Mulk Raj Anand (1905-2004) that his sensitive and youthful fervour was transformed into a comprehensive aesthetic sensibility that combined, as he has himself described the synthesizing philosophy, a "historical humanism" with "existential expressionism" (1949, 4-5). It is crucial to remember that Anand did not remain a mere witness but was a participant in some of the major revolutions, both political and intellectual, that molded the history of the world. It is not surprising that he should invariably draw upon the rich archive of memory that comprised the experiences of his life. This paper explores some of the shaping influences on Anand's philosophy that motivated and empowered his writing and gave it the edge of a social conscience.

About the genesis of his fiction, Anand has explained in different forums that they "arose from a long confession of nearly two thousand pages, which I wrote from the compulsion of a morbid obsession with myself and the people who possessed me, deep in my conscience" (1968, 17). The autobiographical inspiration of his narrative art is repeatedly emphasized. He writes, "through many adversities, trials and errors, heart-rending experiences and several breakdowns, the characters from my long confession have become a miscellany of novels and short stories" (1965, 15). Such claims find vindication in the several accounts of his childhood, youth and adulthood.

Mulk Raj Anand was born in Peshawar as the son of Lal Chand, a coppersmith and soldier, and Ishwar Kaur. The family belonged to the Kshatriya caste that is the warrior class according to the ancient *varnasrama*. Thus, to be a fighter was Anand's patrimony and the seeds of rebellion were planted early in his mind. Though a scion of an upper caste family, Anand's preferred playmates were often the children of the sweepers and the servants, the so-called "untouchables" of the Hindu society. In fact, the most memorable character of his novels, Bakha in *Untouchable* (1935) seems to be a composite of Anand's childhood friends. Thus, even as a child Anand was defiantly crossing social boundaries that separated man from man on the basis of caste and creed. Then, as an undergraduate student at the University of Panjab, Amritsar, Anand witnessed the bloody aftermath of the Jallianwala Bagh massacre (1919) and tasted the cruelty of imperialism when he received eleven lashes and a short prison sentence for joining Gandhi's protest movement. The persistent resistance to any form of imperialism that manifests itself later in his writing would be drawn from these experiences.

Partly to escape further arrest, but also to avoid the bourgeois ambitions of his soldier father, Anand decided to pursue further studies in England. With encouragement and material support from his mother and the principal of his college, the famous poet Iqbal, Anand joined the University College, London in the autumn of 1925. Unlike other Indian students at the time who came from affluent families, he had to work in Indian restaurants and later for a publishing firm to earn his keep.

A year after he arrived in London, the 1926 General Strike took place which was to have a profound effect upon him. Anand's natural sympathies were with the strikers and he found himself comparing the position of the English worker with that of Indians under colonial rule and found the British governance seriously lacking. His indignation at the way the state treated the strikers was outstripped only by his outrage at the attitudes of the majority of his fellow students who were eager to scab and volunteer to help run trains, trams and tubes to make the strike ineffective. Anand saw this as treachery and promptly associated himself with a small group of students who "refused to be bullied by the others". For his pains he was attacked in Gower Street by a group of 'loyalist' students. But he had no regrets and declared that "in life there are some things worth getting beaten up for" (1946, 53-54).

As he worked towards his doctoral degree, he sought opportunities to socialize with like-minded liberals and intellectuals. London at that time was the centre of the English-speaking intellectual world and Anand soon joined the literary circle known as the 'Bloomsbury group'. Here he met writers such as T.S. Eliot, Leonard and Virginia Woolf, E.M. Forster, H.G. Wells, John Strachey and George Orwell among many others. This class of the literary elite both impressed him and left him feeling perplexed and uncomfortable. To his surprise he discovered that writers whom he held in high esteem were insensitive to the matter of colonialism. For instance, he learnt to his consternation that according to Eliot, Gandhi was an 'anarchist' and that Indians should concentrate on cultural aspects of their society and leave the politics of governance to the British! Though such sentiments were hardly unexpected from T.S. Eliot who by his own admission was "a Classicist in literature, a Royalist in politics, and Anglo-Catholic in religion", they served to disillusion Anand about the literary elite in England. Many of these writers had never visited India and based their impressions upon orientalist writings and/or nineteenth century romantic stories like Rudyard Kipling's *Kim*, which to Anand was typical of the colonial fantasies about India. But that did not stop them from making pompous statements on a subject about which they knew so little. Thus, this early period of Anand's London sojourn was rather like a *rite de passage* which taught him not to compromise his values and forsake the spirit of resistance either to appease his friends in a foreign land or in awe of reputation.

But fortunately not all writers were as parochial as Eliot. Anand found himself drawn to the Woolfs and, more importantly, to E.M. Forster with whom there developed an enduring friendship [Forster wrote the Preface to Anand's

Untouchable to fulfil the condition laid down by the twentieth publisher, after the manuscript had been earlier rejected by nineteen others]. Anand regarded Forster's *A Passage to India* as a sensitive novel on his homeland that went beyond the orientalist conceptions of the 'natives' and attempted to depict the complex, often contradictory and mostly confrontational impact of colonial rule in India.

Another influence on Anand at this time was his acquaintance with the nationalist struggle in Ireland and the writing of the Irish that was infused with the spirit of Irish nationalism. He read James Joyce's novels, especially *The Portrait of the Artist as a Young Man* and *Ulysses*, and the poems of Yeats that found an echo in his heart. Anand visited Ireland in 1927 and became convinced that he too would write—there was no doubt in his mind that he would eventually write—about the lives of the ordinary folk and their struggle against adversities that were the result of political and social imperialism, economic exploitation, or *la condition humane*.

Anand's sympathies with nationalist struggles drew him inevitably to the Spanish Civil War (1936-39) as a soldier volunteer in the "International Brigades" fighting the fascist forces. The Spanish Civil War was a very complicated war (in terms of issues and factions) that was the culmination of a prolonged period of political unrest in a country that was increasingly polarized and repeatedly unable to ameliorate the conditions of terrible poverty of its people. Spain was a country in which landless peasants cobbled together a bare subsistence by following the harvests on vast agricultural estates of wealthy landowners. The tragedy was compounded by the fact that the hierarchical Catholic Church preferred to ally itself with the rich. In a progressively fracturing social order, the military came to see itself, rather melodramatically, as the only bulwark against civil disorder and as the ultimate guarantor of the core values of Spanish society. What the military did not anticipate, however, was the determined resistance of the Spanish people against a military coup. When the military realized they were not going to win by fight against their own people, they appealed to fascist dictatorships in Italy, Germany, and Portugal for assistance and soon began receiving both men and supplies from Benito Mussolini, Adolf Hitler and Antonio Salazar. Fighting groups such as "Escuadrilla España" and the "International Brigades" were spontaneously formed and volunteers came from all over Europe and America (including writers like Ernest Hemingway and Andre Malraux. Pablo Picasso's famous painting *Guernica 1937* reflects the horrors of the civil war) to support the Spanish peasantry in its fight against the fascist forces.

The grim life of the Spanish people must have served as a vivid reminder to Anand of the sufferings of his own people chafing against the yoke of colonialism. Strong would have been his memories of the Amritsar massacres and the systematic depletion of his country's resources resulting in the human agency-induced famines, the most terrifying being that of 1942, that led to dehumanizing deprivations for the people. It is hardly surprising that such subjects should urge passionate articulation. The memories of his participation in the Spanish Civil War were documented by Ernest Hemingway in his unforgettable fiction *For Whom the Bell Tolls* and *Stories of the Spanish Civil War*. For Anand, those memories fed his furious indignation, his social protest and his ideology, which when expressed later in his fiction, often undiluted and undigested through fictional plotting and characterization, were panned by critics as doctrinaire propaganda (Walsh, 63-67; Berry, 94-96). Critics observe that Anand's commitment to his ideology often overpowers the detachment that a creative writer should develop towards his writing, which in turn prevents the smooth transmutation of information into the aesthetic substance of his fiction. Margaret Berry faults him for being "technically unable to cope with the dangers to art of 'writing for a cause'" (95).

Anand lived in England for about twenty-one years and lectured intermittently between 1932 and 1945 at the Workers Educational Association in London and in a likewise manner at the League of Nations School of Intellectual Cooperation in Geneva. As the Second World War enveloped the whole of Europe, Anand became a broadcaster and scriptwriter in the film division of the BBC in London. But travelling in Europe brought him into contact with a group of politically sensitized litterateurs, which was destined to leave an indelible mark not only on Anand's philosophy but upon India's political and intellectual life.

The *Congress for the Defense of Culture* was held in Paris in 1935 and attracted transnational representation, which included intellectuals and writers of international significance like Maxim Gorky, Andre Gide, Andre Malraux, Romain Rolland, Thomas Mann, Heinrich Mann, Henri Barbusse, Aldous Huxley, Feuchtwanger. The congregation defined the need for a transnational cohort to collectively defend Reason, Humanism and Culture from barbaric assaults. Similarly, *International Congress of Writers* was held in Paris and London in 1935 and again at Madrid in 1936. The spirit of these conferences was to build a collective intellectual resistance against the fascist designs and the mortal danger those designs held for humanity. The message achieved further urgency in the 1944 *Paris Anti-fascist Conference* when the members pledged to counter the fascist atrocities and put their pen to exhortative use. Most of the intellectuals of the group sought to think through new versions of identity that ignored ethnic particularities in stark contrast to the Nazis who, in their counterpoised characterization represented Unreason (or an obtuse irrationality) and Barbarity.

Anand was invited to represent India at the *World Congress of Writers* at Paris and at Madrid in 1935. It is to his immense credit that Mulk Raj Anand brought home with him the basic ideas of political and cultural revolution and sought to transplant those ideas of liberalism and social equality among his own people.

Initially, on his return to London, along with a fellow writer Sajjad Zaheer, Anand set up the All-India Progressive Writers' Association (AIPWA) in 1935. He wrote the first draft of their manifesto which with minor adjustments was adopted at the first conference of the association held in Lucknow, India, in April 1936 under the Presidentship of Munshi Premchand. According to Anand, Sardar Jafri and poets Faiz Ahmed Faiz and Majaz Lakhnavi were the moving spirits behind the

Progressive Movement as far as Urdu literature was concerned. Soon, literary figures from other languages, such as Umashankar Joshi (Gujarati), K. Shivarama Karanth (Kannada), Tarashankar Banerjee (Bengali), Sumitranandan Pant and Suryakant Tripathi 'Nirala' (Hindi) joined the movement. The eminent Malayalam poet Vallathol Narayana Menon was its patron and Jawaharlal Nehru, Sarojini Naidu and Rabindranath Tagore attended some of the conferences. Younger poets like Kaifi Azmi, Sahir Ludhianvi, Majrooh Sultanpuri, Firaq Gorakhpuri and fiction writers such as Ismat Chugtai, Krishan Chander and Rajinder Singh Bedi entered its fold later.

AIPWA was a pan-Indian organisation that represented the major linguistic sectors, was staunchly secular in outlook and politically committed to fight for an independent and united India which would ensure social justice and equality for its entire people. At its height, AIPWA probably had over 30,000 members writing literature in all the Indian 'vernaculars'. What bound all these writers together was their non-compromising spirit of rebellion against the evils of the prevailing social system, conventional morality and India's dependence on Britain. As far as aesthetic ideals were concerned, the movement took its lead from a passage in Munshi Premchand's presidential address at the Lucknow conference that gave the clarion call: *We have to change the criteria of beauty.*

That this literary association was also a social and political movement closely aligned to the Communist Party of India and influenced by Nehruvian nationalism is to Anand's credit. Though he never failed to acknowledge Marx's *Das Capital* and Engels' *Anti-Duhring* for providing him with the philosophical basis for the conduct of his life, he did not call himself a Marxist or a Leninist; preferring to rather remain a 'rational humanist'. Neither did he join the Communist Party, always joking that the party would never be able to tolerate him. But he was very much a 'fellow traveller', aligning himself with the best elements of the left tradition in India.

Anand's creative career was launched in 1935 when he completed the first and subsequently hailed as a pathbreaking novel, *Untouchable.* It is an admirable debut novel and reflects the precipitation of all his experiences and beliefs. Not only did the novel go through the expected birthpangs, it underwent a radical metaphorphosis in response to Gandhi's comments. During this period, Anand was dividing his time between the literary London and Gandhi's India. He was profoundly influenced by Gandhian philosophy and visited the Mahatma frequently. As the story goes, he came one day to Gandhi's ashram dressed like a typical Englishman in corduroys, silk tie and suede shoes carrying a draft of his manuscript. Gandhi advised him to stop 'dressing like a monkey' (i.e. like an undiscriminating mimic of the West, not able to understand the demands of the Indian climate conditions) and not let "[his] untouchables sound too much like Bloomsbury intellectuals...[for instance] an untouchable boy wouldn't talk in those long sentences." Anand took Gandhi's correction to heart and re-wrote the entire novel.

The heuristic impact of the novel need not be stressed. Placed in its own context, the novel was unique in many ways, the most important being the choice of the subaltern as the protagonist. A number of other novels followed in quick succession, all exploring the Indian subaltern in the realistic mode: *Coolie* (1936), *Two Leaves and a Bud* (1937), *The Village* (1939), *Across the Black Waters* (1941), *The Sword and the Sickle* (1942), *The Old Woman and the Cow* (1960), and *The Road* (1961).

These novels work within the same grid, with stereotypical characterization presenting protagonists as victim-heroes and other characters as either saviors or oppressors, almost 'Victorian' (Walsh, 67) in their structure, treatment and style. Each story tracks the anguished lives of the protagonists groping in the darkness of *karma* and *varna* for a justification for the ignominy of discrimination, exploitation and oppression they helplessly suffer and have suffered for generations. Each story is a sincere attempt to describe the social and economic injustices that the normative society meets out to a particular class of people in the name of *dharma*; yet without whom the society cannot function. Those of this class, designated *shudras* in the *varnasrama*, perform the basest, the dirtiest and the most ill-paid chores and through their agency is the body of the society kept functional and clean. But for the work that they do, they are pushed to the margin of the very same social body and are stamped with the stigma of being 'polluted' and therefore 'untouchable' or are treated to the dregs of social benefits.

Committed as Anand was to the ideal of a united India, he realized early and with discerning accuracy that the fragmented polity of the country must first be mended to build a healthy nation. His creative work was intended towards refining such awareness. He warns that "We must see ourselves as we are, struggling out of the days of contempt of the caste orders, emancipating our minds from the submission to one man rule, we are dimly becoming aware of the nature of our hopeless resignation in the past to unknown fate..." (1949:5). He writes to be taken seriously and remains passionate about his ideology. He believes in propagating 'art with a purpose' and has gone on record for celebrating "All art as propaganda." He declares "The art of Ajanta is propaganda for Buddhism. The art of Ellora is propaganda for Hinduism..." and so on (Walsh, 63). Anand claims that his mission is to paint the grim picture of the life of the downtrodden and also suggest the possible methods of alleviation of their suffering. His lifelong commitment to social reform as the process of historical evolution urges him to make the regenerative spirit intrinsic to his art. In his view, the artist/writer bears a responsibility to the society and has to perform a task "of destroying the spurious elements of contemporary civilization or of reconstructing the future society" (1946:136). Any attempt to "shirk" such a responsibility is "a betrayal of his own powers and the acceptance of mental and spiritual death. Above all, it is a betrayal of the common humanity to which he is committed as an individual born to live in community with other individuals, a denial of all human relations, a secession from society" (1946, 136). Anand sets very high ideals indeed for making the function of writing a kind of social activism. He wants his own writing to reflect "the wisdom of the heart" while addressing the "naked truth of human life in India" (Cowasjee, 115).

Credit must be given where it is due. Anand has scored

many firsts. Echoing Premchand's dictum of defining new standards of 'beauty' by locating it in the struggles of the dis-privileged, Anand has created paradigms like a Bakha, Munnoo and Gauri with a kind of existential expressionism to convey the authenticity of their living conditions and idiom to measure "against the fantastic Kim" (Cowasjee, 116). Whatever the aesthetic limitations of Anand's prose it nonetheless, with its close attention to the surface of life in pre-Independence India, affords the reader a clear view of his characters and their world. The subaltern protagonists operate as the episteme in the entire body of his writing. No one could have imagined, dared or even risked (bearing the marketability of the books in mind) choosing such protagonists as he did as heroes. By giving them fictional life, Anand ensured their enduring presence in literary discourse.

He goes even further. Indian historiography would not be complete, Anand justifiably claims, until the subaltern is given his rightful place in it. The short story titled "The Barbers' Trade Union" opens thus: "Among the makers of modern India, Chandu, the barber boy of our village, has a place which will be denied him unless I press for the recognition of his contribution to history." The narrative voice is almost undistinguishable from the author's own and Anand, just as he writes in the story, takes upon himself in a peremptory manner the task of speaking for the socially inarticulate as well as the onerous responsibility of writing them into the Indian historiography. He might hence be accused—and has frequently been—of being presumptive. But there is no doubt that his intentions are honourable. He does delve into the subaltern psyche and describe the pain and sorrow, certainly for the first time in Indian novels written in English. Undoubtedly, his novels anticipate, may have even quickened the process of, the subalterns speaking for themselves and becoming the subject of their own narratives.

Anand has received adulation as well as his own share of disparagement; lately, even neglect. The criticism has been mostly directed at his exhortatory and ideology-driven rhetoric. The obtrusive preaching has often been described as unpalatable and seriously impeding his style of writing. Critics have called him "a thirties man" for not changing his views and remaining in the reformatory groove of the early decades of pre-Independence India. Fifty-five years after Independence and in the light of the Dalit writing that has emerged, Mulk Raj Anand may appear either too naïve or too authoritative. The significance of his writing may have progressively diminished. But his contribution to the body of Indian literature and the shaping of the social ethos of the nation cannot be forgotten. He may be the least known Indian novelist today in the West. This may partly be because his politics and socialism are not fashionable and partly because his style lacks the finesse and flair of the leading writers of Indian English today. When he was alive, Anand took the verbal battery of the critics as stoically as he had borne the assaults of the pro-Establishment students in Gower Street, London. He was a prolific writer and wrote to reiterate his philosophy, never compromising his stance at all. He lived and died an unrepentant non-conformist and an unwavering ideologue, following in his life the principles he preached in his writing. For example, despite the existence of a fine cottage on his verdant five-acre plot in Khandala (near Mumbai), where he spent the last years of his life, Anand chose to live in one of the out-houses on his property in a spartan way. On his death, his property is willed to the Sarvodaya Trust, a charitable non-profit organization devoted to the promotion of Gandhian ideals.

Since human suffering is a universal phenomenon, the warmth of Anand's simple, moving, humane narratives will never fail to stir the heart-strings of the sensitive reader. But as someone has rightly observed, literature with reformative zeal is not likely to remain objective. Anand did not succeed in dissociating his sensibility from his work. Perhaps he did not wish to. He wanted his writing to be the instrument of his social activism. And in that he has achieved unqualified success.

REFERENCES

Anand, Mulk Raj. *Apology for Heroism: A Brief Autobiography of Ideas.* Delhi: Kutub-Popular, 1946.

——. "Prolegomena to a New Humanism", *Lines Written to an Indian Air.* Bombay: Nalanda Publications, 1949.

——. "How I became a Writer", *Contemporary Indian Literature*. Vol. V, Nos. 11-12 (Nov.-Dec.), 1965 .

——. "The Story of my Experiment with a White Lie", *Critical Essays in Indian Writing in English*. Ed. M.K. Naik et al. Dharwar: Karnatak University, 1968.

——. "Why I Write?" *Perspectives on Mulk Raj Anand*. Ed. K.K. Sharma. Ghaziabad: Vimal Prakashan, 1978.

Berry, Margaret. *Mulk Raj Anand: The Man and the Novelist*. Amsterdam: Oriental Press, 1971.

Cowasjee, Saros, Ed. *Author to Critic: The Letters of Mulk Raj Anand to Saros Cowasjee*. Calcutta: Writers Workshop, 1973.

Walsh, William. *Indian Literature in English*. London & New York: Longman, 1990.

Towards a Closer Understanding of Anand

7

G.S. Balram Gupta

An Indian critic of considerable reputation once referred to Mulk Raj Anand as "an extinct volcano", but for all we know, Anand has belied the critic's verdict by continuing to remain active—creatively and otherwise too. In fact, during the course of an informal conversation with a host of admiring delegates at the fourth triennial ACLALS conference (held at Delhi from 2nd to 8th January, 1977), Anand asserted in his usual ebullient fashion: "If you ask me why I write so many novels, I say it's because I love!" Though on the face of it the statement may look in no way extraordinary, I believe if offers a sure clue to a clear understanding of not only Anand's novels and other writings but to that of his entire personality and philosophy. It is this love—not for oneself or one's own, but for the entire mankind, transcending all constricting limitations of caste, creed, and economic or social status, and all geographical boundaries of nations all of which are man-made—that is at the root of Anand's philosophy which animates all his activities, including his prolific writing. In his *The Swan and the Eagle* Professor C.D. Narasimhaiah has rightly emphasized "the human centrality" of Anand's fiction, but it needs to be recognized that that forms the very core of Anand's philosophy as well.

Anand's position today, despite his determined detractors, is absolutely secure as one of the doyens of Indian Writing in English. Scholarly research work continues to be done on him, both here and abroad, and more and more critical works on his life and literature have been coming out. However, I am afraid we do not as yet have even a single authentic biographical-critical study of Anand comprehensive enough to cover all the aspects of his multi-faceted genius. I am aware of the problems involved in an attempt like this. After all, Anand is a unique personality. Were he merely a fictional writer that would be no great problem: but the roles he assumes are different and various. He has been a professor, a social worker, a pacifist, an educationist, an art critic, a critic of dance, music, painting, sculpture, and so on. Naturally, anyone who attempts a standard, all-comprehensive study of Anand has got to be not merely a critic of literature, but several things more. Anyway, while I hope that some day such a study will come out, I wish to insist here on the fact that the most pertinent and fruitful way of approaching the subject would be to consider Anand's life and personality, and all his writings of which even now we do not have a complete and authentic bibliography, in the light of his philosophy of humanism which has been the fountain-head of all his thinking, acting, and writing.

Though he began as a student of Locke, Berkeley, and Hume, eventually Anand realized the futility of accepting any faith postulated by others. So, refusing to espouse any ready-made philosophy, either of the East or of the West, during the long period of his chequered career which has been for him a chain of challenges and a series of quests, Anand has come to evolve for himself what he calls "comprehensive historical humanism" which is a synthesis of several Oriental as well as Occidental brands of humanism, a synthesis which aims at finding solutions to the myriad problems of man in these tragic, sordid, broken times. The essence of this confessedly eclectic humanism was in a way stated long ago by the Greek philosopher, Protagoras: "Man is the measure of all things."

What I propose to do in this article is by no means to give any systematic account of Anand's philosophy of humanism, but I shall just try to throw some light on some of its important aspects, and their relevance to Anand's work, basing the entire thing mainly on some excerpts drawn from his own communications to me. Obviously, one may not find much coherence here, but nonetheless, I hope it will be of sufficient use to those who may want to have some intimate insights into Anand, the man, and Anand, the humanist.

It has by now unfortunately become a commonplace fashion in critical circles to denounce and dismiss Anand as a "committed writer", as though it were possible for any great writer worth the name not to be at all committed to some set of values of philosophy of life. The moot point to be noted about Anand is that he has always firmly believed in the role of a writer as essentially a crusader in the cause of Humanity: no hotch-potch of Vedantism, no hazy mysticism, but an inalienable faith in man. Art, philosophy, religion, science, and all other similar systems and faculties are naught if they are not geared up to the service of mankind. Thus, it has been one of Anand's deep-rooted convictions that literature, far from being for its own sake, is for the sake of man, for refining and ennobling him, for stirring up the dormant stores of tenderness in him for his fellow human beings and for inspiring him into action calculated to achieve the well-being of the mankind as a whole. It is precisely for this reason we find that Anand is no spinner of fairy tales for mere amusement or a fabricator of escapist literature. On the contrary, he has always written to emphasise the essential dignity of man—despite his weaknesses—and to engender compassion in the hearts of men for the oppressed and the downtrodden. In a conversation with me Anand once averred: "My books are like so many flames: and that explains why they are being translated in so many countries." And of what use if a book if it will not result in wisdom which, in turn, ought to lead us to action? If only to substantiate this, let me quote Bulwer-Lytton: "Books are but waste paper unless we spend in action the wisdom we get from thought." Viewed in this light, most of Anand's books have enjoyed unquestionable success. Here is Anand feeling rightfully comforted at the influence that his novels *Coolie* and *Untouchable* (incidentally, these two are the most largely translated of Anand's novels) have exerted on thinking men the entire world over:

> You will be reassured to know that many young Africans are reading me and feel that I confirm their familiar feelings. The greatest moment for me was when

> the Angolian poet, Augustino Netto, who had come from the middle of a battle for the liberation of his country, to read a poem in Algiers, told me that he had been inspired once to go into action by my book *Coolie*. In the dynamic world outside India, the human situation confronted by me has already meaning.
>
> Stalkey Carmichael of the Black Power Movement told me that his will to murder all the whites of America was stayed by the novel *Untouchable*. (1969, 6 August)

In fact, I have always felt—and I am confident those that have even a little acquaintance with Anand will concur with me—that what distinguishes Anand primarily from other contemporary Indian writers in English is that he has always believed that ideas are nothing unless, they are translated into action. And he has always practised what he has thought it fit to preach. Whether he is writing or lecturing or touring, he never loses sight of his deep concern for the suffering mankind. This is how this globetrotter accounts for his frequent tours:

> I returned from abroad this morning and go off again, at the end of next week, for another twelve days.
>
> You will wonder why these frequent trips have to be undertaken. I asked myself this question, during my last journey in Kazakhstan. I find that the intelligentsia of the world outside India is deeply anxious to create new friendships to communicate at the intensest level of human solidarity and deep consciousness of the struggle of man everywhere to fight against those who wish to separate the new young peoples, and to throt their hopes and aspirations. One hundred writers, intellectuals, and scientists, under my chairmanship, went on record against the war in Vietnam and quite a few governments have recognized the new provisional government of the liberation movement. I only wish our countryman would try to combine ideas and actions and help to liberate the millions of our people from the frustrations placed in their way by those who have inherited superiorities. (1969, 11 July)

That way, Anand has never been guilty of confining himself to any sort of ivory tower. He is too honest and conscientious a soul to go on doing smart writing on privation and poverty without ever concretely bothering to remove them. A first rank intellectual, Anand has always loved to put in physical labour for the relief of the poor and the unfortunate. The following excerpts may throw enough light on the truth of my statement:

> I find myself involved in relief work in the Maharashtra famine areas and feel, at the end of it all, that my obsession with people in the writings has been justified by the contemporary history of ruin and disaster which has been brought upon us mainly by the crimes of the political intelligentsia. If we had all spoken of the vast scarcity and the insecurities of many kinds which have come within the bereftness, we might have been able to extend our own consciousness as also to invoke *karuna* from which alone any literature can be justified.... I can tell you that what is significant in our time is the assertion of love for human beings, specially in their own weaknesses, in the dignity of their frailty and in the utter wretchedness. (1973, 14 August)

Literature is important. But that is not everything. It is only a means to an end. And often there are times when action needs to be given priority over literature. Nearly a month after the last communication had arrived, Anand wrote:

> I am afraid things are so bad in regard to food in our country, that the condition of man has degenerated especially in Maharashtra. I am spending my time not writing, but doing relief work. (1973, 13 September)

Anand's life has been an incessant struggle, characterized by a fearless protest against inhumanity and a boundless compassion for man. Tenderness or '*karuna*' (as the Enlightened One puts it) is the very essence of Anand's humanism. Once he wrote to say:

> The Chinese philosopher Mencius once said, "A sage is the instructor of hundred ages...." I hope I can teach

> even a few people of my generation that tenderness is our only asset. (1965, 26 August)

It sounds rather strange that not only the common man but even well-informed academicians seem to believe that Anand is a thoroughbred Marxist with no relevance to the aspirations of the people of his country. Nothing could be farther from truth. While it is true that Marx is one of the several intellectuals who have influenced Anand considerably, it is most proper to regard him only as a humanist. Here is Anand's own clarification:

> I believe Marx supplies a good yardstick for history and his basic proposition "Means of production determine consciousness" is correct. Except that Marx naturally simplified his thesis. He could not explain the irrational, instinctive and intuitive actions of man. There are many areas like aesthetic activity he left out. I am not a member of any political party. I reject nothing that is human. I agree with Coomaraswamy when he said: "Civilization must henceforth be human rather than local or national, or else it cannot exist." (1968, 4 August)

Even with regard to his conviction about the concepts of religion and God he is quite categorical. About the former, he says:

> I do not believe in institutionalized religion. And like Tolstoy, I would like to leave the beliefs of people to their private conscience, collaborating with them for certain secular ends, without objecting to their pet religions. (1968, 4 August)

And here is Anand's cryptic quip about God:

> God has been dead a long time. Men are gods, or can become gods. (1967, 12 July)

This, obviously, is a courageous statement born of no amorphous conviction, and the following letter, I believe, throws a little more light on the issue:

> One of the concerns I shared with other humanists like Babbitt and romantics like Murray was the question of restraint. Much as I wanted the breakdown of our

> orthodoxy, I did not want lack of restraint in man. I wanted freedom on all the planes, but not libertinism. I wanted tenderness in sex, but not the violence of sadism which have been let loose in Europe and America by the permissive society. I wanted grace in human relations without the belief in god, but did not want to destroy contemplativeness. In fact, somewhere I have asked for a religion without religion. I wanted friendship and imagination like Morgan Forster but much more from the pervasive love of Rumi, Hafiz and Iqbal.... (1972, 21 March)

However, though it may sound a paradox, it appears to be true that Anand's interest in man—with his strengths and weaknesses, his struggles and defeats or triumphs—is more important for him than a construction of any regular, systematic philosophy about him. Here is Anand's own assertion about it:

> The concern with man's destiny in my case is not in a positive, rationalistic and scientific manner. In fact, when I sleep well, I can't write the next morning. I am really interested in the inner struggle, through confusion, unrest and chaos, of men and women to break through, from themselves and their weaknesses. In this sense, the weaknesses are important as the sources of strength. And when these characters are able to confront their own hatred, fear, cruelty and cowardice, they show what man can be. Death in my novels is the tragic" moment of life, from which hope can be born....
>
> It (*Morning Face*) is on the same lines as an essay in epic-myth as Raja Rao's *The Serpent and the Rope*. Only different in the sense of values, because I do not believe in any one system of philosophy, but in the wisdom of the heart. (1969, 8 November)

In the ultimate analysis, Anand appears to believe in this "wisdom of the heart" rather than in any formal philosophy. While offering his frank remarks on my review of his *Morning Face* (with which, incidentally, he was not much satisfied) he wrote:

> There is no story in it (*Morning Face*), there is only a pattern, to give room for vibrations. Please begin to study the interior life of human beings in my books and bring out their fundamental essences. Don't look to the philosophy, but try to look for the wisdom of the heart. I am not Raja Rao. Nor am I R.K. Narayan. I see divinity in each object, each flower, each animal, each human being, and I am looking for the *quick* as the mystics look for *illumination*. (1970, 3 February)

I received a similar exhortation in yet another letter:

> I beg you to go into the humanness of the character, see the things in between and then philosophise...read the novels for the "wisdom of the heart" and not for the system of humanism.... Do try and become a sensitive outsider, a human being, and not a systematic philosopher. (1970, 3 March)

These are revealing statements indeed. They go to establish Anand's overriding concern for man over and above any systematic philosophy. I may as well quote from another of his letters wherein he states his position with all possible force and clarity:

> I did not write tracts on humanism, but have written about human beings.... (1971, 8 January)

Agreed. But I don't think Anand refutes my contention that it is impossible to separate a man's creative writings from his philosophy. A thorough knowledge of the latter is a sure help for a deep insight into the former. For that matter, I believe it is high time Anand came out with his treatise on his philosophy of humanism the ideas of which are now found scattered in some of his stray articles and his *Apology for Heroism*, if only because we would then be in a better position to relate his life to his writings, and his philosophy to his enormous work in areas other than creative writing. We ought to be cautious of those critics with whom it is fashionable to say that they care for the writing, not for the writer, as though there could ever be one without the other.

As I have remarked earlier, it is not enough if we have half-a-dozen studies and of Anand with sketchy descriptions of his life and intelligent discussions of his fiction. Anand's creative work, it is true, is quite enormous. But no critical work on him can be deemed thoroughly complete unless it takes into consideration his various other books and articles on fine arts, culture, education, politics, and so on, plus the practical efforts he has been tirelessly putting forth in the great cause of international peace and amity, and in that of the welfare of man in general.

REFERENCES

Mulk Raj Anand's Letters to the Author:

Letter, dated 26 August 1965.

——, dated 12 July 1967.

Anand's reply to a questionnaire: 4 August 1968.

Letter, dated 11 July 1969.

——, dated 6 August 1969 (written just after his participation in the first Pan African Cultural Festival at Algiers).

——, dated 8 November 1969.

——, dated 3 February 1970.

——, dated 3 March 1970.

——, dated 8 January 1971.

——, dated 21 March 1972.

——, dated 14 August 1973.

——, dated 13 September 1973.

Mulk Raj Anand: The Crusader as the Creator

8

Binod Mishra

Indian Writing in English today has become a literary firmament where innumerable stars twinkle every night and help each other shine. These stars have provided much light to enable the beneficiaries to understand the "complexities of Indian life, which is getting transformed very fast under the impact of forces from all over the world since independence" (Maheshwari, 2002, Preface). But the attempt to bring out the camouflaged crises enveloping Indian masses and the mind was agog in its pre-independent days too. Mulk Raj Anand, one of the three pioneers of Indian Writing in English led this movement with a charismatic zeal to portray the penury and the predicament of common man in India crushed and trampled under the demoniac yoke debarring man from his fellow beings in the name of petty man-made dichotomies. K.R.S. Iyengar in his seminal book on Indian Writing does not exaggerate to find 'stamina and stern consistency of purpose' in Mulk Raj Anand and R.K. Narayan (81). The path shown by these stalwarts has become a garden where one can have his stay full of fragrance exuded by flowers of all varieties and the plants planted and nurtured by these precursors.

The present paper is an attempt to show Mulk Raj Anand as an artist. A good number of critics and scholars straitjacket Anand by calling him a writer of sociological novels. Some even label him as a Communist. The present paper makes an exegesis of his masterpiece, *The Bubble* and endeavors to establish Anand not as a crusader but also as a creator.

Anand seems to be a crusader in his early novels. But his Byzantine world offers us reasons galore to be a rebel. He is a rebel not because he wanted to be treated differently rather he's a critic of false notions, practices and orthodox ideas. His fulminations against taboos are the vivid realizations that man has to undergo in the light of changing times and situations. He rebels to reform. Those who consider Anand's work as social documentaries and reject them as literary pieces perhaps forget the fact that a writer, despite telling stories, also has a social responsibility to bring changes and enable mankind to come out of the web and think for green pastures, which symbolize progressive mindsets. Society, like mankind, doesn't remain fixed but it is always in a flux. A society, which sticks to old traditions and orthodox beliefs, cannot welcome change. Change symbolizes dynamism and if we are blind to progress, we cease to be. Anand as a representative of art and literature recorded these changes and also propelled people to think for alternatives. To call any system as the most authentic and reliable deters us from being clairvoyants and if we fail in preparing ourselves for future, we are no men at all.

Anand may be writing in a language that is alien but he maintains his nativity by portraying the conditions prevailing in his motherland. His greatness as a writer can be realized in the depiction of the deplorable condition not only of downtrodden and dejected but also of his decry against the observance of various social taboos troubling mankind. His admiration for his kinship with nation can be best understood in his attempt to defy alien rule and domination in their own language. English as a medium of his writing provided him with a weapon to fight the irrepressible ennui of his people yoked to a horrendous subjugation. English language as a more common link between a nation and the world attracted worldwide attention towards India's devastating condition. Love to one's nation cannot be confined to writing only in one's mother tongue. A true writer is also responsible for bringing change in a society if it goes off-track. Indian writers, through their writing have familiarized the world with Indian myths and traditions, possibilities and probabilities, relativities and realities and Anand stands at the fountainhead of all with his awe inspiring gems in the form of sketches, short stories and novels.

The heroes in Anand's early novels, although downtrodden and debased as per social canons are not debilitated. They want to throw challenge to the orthodox established practices. Anand portrays social stigma by depicting the social incidents in their lives. Bakha, Munoo and Gangu remind the privileged classes of society that the same clay moulds them and the same blood runs through their veins. If Providence didn't have any discrimination in shaping them, segregation made by man was really questionable. Anand criticizes these man-made divisions and wants them to be abolished. The caste system also emphasizes spiritual crises. This crisis can be overcome by breaking all barriers and considering people of all castes to be one. The appearance of Mahatma Gandhi is symbolic of change that the saint will vouchsafe to ignorant mankind.

Anand's first phase as a novelist is full of revolutionary radicalism and as he grows, his novels, his characters also graduate to accommodate everything yet fighting to free from the clutches and listen to the musings of the heart. The crusader of yesteryears had to construct a new order to help mankind.

Mulk Raj Anand remained true to his mission of writing. His personal life bears an indelible imprint on his writing. He disliked his father for his fealty to the British government. His mother's invocation to idols, at times made him too sensitive. The contrary pulls of his parents generated in him a tension. His early days in a world materially poor and spiritually limited made him a non-conformist who hated the gap between the actual and the ideal. He also suffered the tedium of an empty and banal life 'where growth and self-awareness were thwarted'. His mission of life to redeem reality through art took him to England where his literary journey began and he emerged as one of the leading novelists of his time.

Anand's description of social issues has caused many critics to call him as a period novelist. A period novelist only illustrates society and doesn't recreate. Anand as a novelist transforms his contingent sense of life into a positive image and provides progressions, which are passionate, and the novel is for him an exploration of human emotions in its most rigorous form. His realism is inalienable from man's romantic will. His art integrates various emotions and impulses without yielding to love of isolationalism. His crusade nature cannot restrict his creative urge. His creative process involves his body and soul, his conscious and unconscious selves. His fiction is not devoid of amorphous urges and it includes a process of distillation, which orients it towards delight.

Anand is a crusader and a creator in the sense that he was aware of his own responsibility as a writer. His technique also differs from Western writers. His writing has its Indian ethos. The Western influences are not strong enough to compel him to play the sedulous ape. He shows the drama of revolt, no doubt, but he also extends the bounds of human empire. Instead of surrendering to the original passion, he chastens and purifies our emotions. The whole man and the whole gamut of his emotions and ties is Anand's preoccupation as an artist. Art for Anand is an illuminating factor.

Anand as a novelist was no slave to conceptualization like D.H. Lawrence. Conceptualization is a prison house, which blurs the artist's vision. It obfuscates and hinders the writer from tracing the twists of the human heart. Anand was also a follower of Virginia Woolf who considered bondage of any kind as irksome. The novel, according to Lawrence, should remain unfathomable. The non-human inhumanity interested both Lawrence and Anand. The passionate subconscious of man is an ego that lives darkly in man's blood and bones. Much like Lawrence, Anand gives us some palpitating moments and takes the reader out of the emotional rut.

Anand's internationally acclaimed novel *The Bubble* is a quintessence of innocence and experience. The novel is more of an autobiography and it is in the form of letters, diary entries and has beautiful titles to all the nine parts. The novel is a beautiful blend of crusader's cantankerous past and creator's yearning to absorb everything by becoming more than himself. Much after knowledge and experience the hero of the novel Krishan looks forward to annex himself to his native roots. Exhausted with his split existence in England, Krishan is determined to gather the new sensations in England for his self-discovery.

Krishan is not an appreciator of Gautama who advocated effacement of the self. Nirvana, according to Krishan, reflects the state of nothingness. Krishan believes in the evolutionary process of life and considers love, hate, adversity and death as the facts of existence. What he writes in a letter to his friend, Noor, is not only Krishan's consciousness but also Anand's sheer exuberance and zest for life:

> The wish to move forward filled me with warmth that urged me on. I wanted to live to breathe, to expound my soul to run wild. (81)

Serious readers and critics find Anand's autobiographical novels as dramatization of soul-searching. There is an unceasing exploration in these novels. Anand himself also considered fiction to be much more than self-analysis. *The Bubble* combines the outward and the inward. Behind the drama of sensual gratification also lies. The spiritual growth of Krishan, various selves are like the seven colours of the rainbow. Life has a complex pattern and an artist has to save himself from being lost in this intricacy. Anand's observations give us a clue to his image of a creator who accommodates as wide range of concerns and perceptions:

> May be the novelist in me will be able to absorb everything better than if I should become a Plato, Hegel or Kant. (574)

The first part of *The Bubble* has Prof. Dicks as the guiding spirit. Krishan learns from him what he needed for a total comprehension of human existence. Prof. Dicks awakened in Krishan the desire to understand the deep layers of philosophy, which couldn't be contaminated by theology. Prof. Dicks's gentleness behind the façade of the dogged rationalist made Krishan love and advice. Krishan comes across Evelyn who encouraged him to understand the platonic aspect of man-woman relationship. Krishan voices the true feeling of Anand's grand obsession for woman in the following lines.

> I feel that most Hindus have seldom tried to understand the soul of a woman and we do not know the things they keep hidden in their hearts. (60)

The first part of *The Bubble* shows Krishan's determination to master life. The concluding lines of the first part reflect Anand's cravings for attaining maturity and mastery and his mastery as an artist:

> I feel quite excited about going into the interior into the quiet of the country away from the big noisy, London where I may be able to go further into the unknown and find some purpose and will of my own to master life. (64)

The second part of *The Bubble* shows the hero's longing for the green grass of the fair earth. Krishan finds the landscape of London a gloomy graveyard. Krishan's evolutionary process includes the facts of existence. The crusader recreates himself by creating a new world for him. Anand's revolutionary fervour allows him to inquire and confront more than submit and surrender. Krishan's encounter with Lucy in the second part of the novel is not without its symbolical significance. Lucy is an apostle of innocence and purity and is a bundle of repressed emotions. Krishan is opposed to the repressive frigidity of Lucy. Krishan considers Lucy as part of negation and emptiness symbolized by Buddha and his philosophy fails to sustain the possibilities of an authentic existence. Anand is a creator in the sense that he believes life to assimilate everything. To subscribe to Buddha's view of life as all pain is like terminating life. Suffering is not the 'be and the end all' of life. Suffering is more liberating and it encourages us to look for fresh possibilities. Life is a joyous celebration for Krishan and what he says is not the voice of a crusader but a creator.

> I am anti-Christ. I want the romantic night even if this brings sorrow and melancholy. I shall have to live through the inner chaos. (138)

Those who consider Anand as a crusader perhaps skip the fact that his fiction is a step towards a better tomorrow and not a fractured today. Anand's work has the soothing effect of a balm, which not only tells us to endure the pain but at the same time think of its permanent cure.

The third part of *The Bubble* is a preparatory ground of Krishan's freedom and ascent. Krishan's contact with Irene here makes him a fuller being. Krishan feels lighter and expansive when there is a physical union between the two. Krishan adores Irene's abstract inner self. The wave of emotions repressed by Lucy in the second part of the novel shows an upsurge towards maturity in the third part wherein Krishan becomes more aware. Irene is an ocean of delight and she paves the way to Krishan's purgation of all his injured repressed and camouflaged chimeras. Krishan seems uplifted and feels transcendence from the bogs of anarchic hell to the bubbles and elixirs of harmonious Elysium.

Krishan, like his creator wanted to absorb everything and fill the empty inner space to achieve an authentic existence. His longing for life and his fervour for more life, attempt at expansion of consciousness. Irene's youth and beauty play a catalyst's part in this search for authentic existence. The second part of the novel may appear to many readers and critics as vapid and vulgar because of sensational details but their views are lopsided. They seem to ignore the fact that sensation can be a part of knowledge and exemplary aspiration also. The complex unity of self can be seen as the key to the ultimate unity of being. E.S. Brightman (1985) views it as the point of interaction between the self and the wider realism of nature:

> The principle of personality is one that forbids mere subjectivism because every person refers beyond himself to the world. Every self transcends itself.

The third part of *The Bubble* is remarkable for the primacy of life—force that can be attained through the satisfaction of bodily urges. Bodily urges like our hunger and thirst are the aspects of ultimate reality. Man-woman relationship is not only carnal by nature but also spiritual and civilizational. Anand maintains his integrity as an artist not merely by sketching the savory but also by revealing the unsavory. He maintains his mission as a creator and asseverates that retreat from reality is a denial of his vocation. He portrays the whole truth of life—sin and holiness, beauty and ugliness, love and hate. His fiction is a true record of life with sprinkles of imagination to help mankind face the odds of life not with a lurking fear but with flickering hope. Anand records with conviction and commitment that the force of sex can be transmuted into the highest form of spiritual energy. The cosmic energy stored in human sexuality can be released into human consciousness. The third part of *The Bubble* is a testimony to the fact that man and woman do not overpower and imprison each other rather they liberate each other and coalesce into each other. They lead one another to the eternal bliss called life.

The fourth part of the novel describes Krishan's journey to Paris. This part shows the protagonist turning inward and realizing that the true self resides in burning, melting and shining. He laments that Indian consciousness is in mire but we can lift ourselves to the stars. We can find the crusader in Anand proceeding towards delight of an artist who relies in the philosophy of happiness beyond the pain on the cross. The body must be explored to perfect the soul. The self of the protagonist sacrifices the body to obey the urge of some more basic principles. Life of ideal harmony is not possible without an awareness of the body. The body is a living link with the world and it is more a liberator than a fetter. It identifies and harmonizes us with the universe. The satiation of body opens the temples of soul and enables us to reach the fullness of existence.

The artist in Anand ideates that the romance and dream is not unreal. He allows us to seek a subtler and profounder form of our existence. Krishan in *The Bubble* is the seeker of the self and the spirit. He, at times, goes away from the noise of life to commune with the largeness and peace of nature. The mind of Krishan moves towards the realization of the totality of life. His existence is a metaphor for harmony, joy and illumination. Krishan does not paralyze himself by his grief and unrest. Instead, he does glimpse the 'soul's eternal spaces'. Krishan faces the real world and renews himself through the assertion of his will.

The fifth part of the novel records Krishan's interaction with the literary giants, philosophers and committed Communists. The sixth part of the novel describes Krishan's journey to Ireland where his rejuvenation with Irene makes him more adventurous. Krishan's confabulations with literary lords in Ireland and Krishan's concatenation with Irene help each other transform themselves. Irene purges Krishan and gives him a shove to the bigger realities. The separation from her oozes him, no doubt, yet the artist in Anand enables Krishan to think beyond his selfconscious love at first sight to the world conscious fact:

> I felt dizzy at my incapacity to recapture that mood. It was as though the exuberance of that moment had rumbled away in the dramas through which "he" and "she" had lived. It was as though I was asking how face to face with the void "he" would feel when she would not be in his arms and there would only be the lingering remorse that they had not matured into another spiritual passion than the carnal love for each other. And now we were going in different directions. The longing would always be there. And the affection. The nerves would remain entertained. Perhaps the vital pull of the bodies would become nostalgias the husk of desire, an idea...why not break my resolve? And stay and suffer? Stay with her whom I have created out of an innocent wayward girl into a woman who had decided to live in action. (529)

The seventh part of the novel under the heading 'Journal to Irene' is Krishan's letters, which are drenched in the delight of self-discovery. He calls it journal because he decided to post all the letters together when Irene was released from jail. His interactions with Betrand Russel, T.E. Lawrence and even Prof. Dicks gave him a new courage to know himself and to stand true to his commitment. What he writes in one of his letters to Irene is not devoid of an artist's acknowledgement and a philosopher's intuition:

> We cannot know ourselves. And in the expressions which we absorb all those experiences, which are the stuff of the evolving world floating in the unconscious, which itself disentangles the feelings through the apperceptions. So the creative act is the magic wand.

> Inspired words send distances between the body and soul. (573)

The eighth part of the novel is a letter from his father to Krishan. The letter is full of taunts and torments of an old parent showing concern for their son. The letter charges Krishan with violating his sacred past and also reminds him of his filial responsibilities. Much in a persuasive tone, the father wants the son to forget the fractured past and start life afresh. Krishan answers his father's letter in the ninth part where he argues his case. He clears all the charges and expresses his ambition in the following lines:

> I don't want to pose as a saint or a hero, though I confess I often feel glow of that ambition and must extirpate it. I just want to be a human and recreate tragic lives of our dumb people. (591)

Anand emerges as a creator in *The Bubble* also because of his prototype protagonist, Krishan who develops self-realization. His letter to his father in the ninth part of the novel is a document drenched in distress. He painfully realizes the pinch of father-son relationship as the blood-flecked web of mutual love hate. After a life of hectic academic hunt in England, Krishan's desire of homecoming is creator's cravings for mending walls. His desire to re-integrate himself into the social and cultural life of his country not only reflects his patriotic fervor but also an artist's ardor of completing the pattern, he sketched once.

Much like a creator, Krishan's letter to Irene in the conclusive part of the novel is an assertion of human will. Krishan's wriggles to come out of the maze of customs and traditions, is a creator's cravings for choice. Krishan's love for life was a love affair with life. Krishan, like an artist, hates confinement and he despises bondage of any kind. He doesn't remain fixed and he looks for a journey to meaning and maturity. The lines of the novel bear ample evidence to the artist's love for inventiveness and optimism:

> One must awaken to fresh possibilities latent in the winters decay the opening of the bud into flowers and

> the promise of the coming of luscious fruit on the tree of happiness. (603)

The Bubble establishes Anand's reputation as the literary artist who begins with himself and in the fullness of his creative vision and energy; his ego loses itself in the infinite. The novel is very much an artistic piece, which will defy the ravages of time. It makes us aware of the tremendous human application that transcends place and time. Anand has very potentially seized every situation in its temporal as well as timeless aspects. The element of celebration does not result in the shrinkage of feeling. His keenness to understand the nature of reality through self-exploration and expiation brings him close to modern writers who delineate the cultural and spiritual crises in their works.

Anand's early novels recorded the emasculation of body, mind and soul and *The Bubble* squeezes these experiences to give forth a new vision. The demons in man are to be dominated by gods in him. Man is to be redeemed from the clutches of his own contrivances. Existential truth is the life of soul and spirit larger than many categories of knowledge. It not only opens the way to self-realization but also shows transcendence from the empirical to self-knowledge and finally a leap from the self to the absolute. Man grows out of himself and shifts his center of vision from himself to the universe.

Thus, we find that Anand is more a creator than a constructor in his fiction. Anand's subjectivity has the power of assimilation. He creates ideal form through the inner life. He rises above nature to make his character beautiful. Realism and idealism are mutually dependent even in *The Bubble*. His frank and intrepid acceptance of existence makes the novel a seminal work of art. The writer's soul breathes life into the material and Anand's acute personal compassion makes no subject matter repulsive for an artist like Anand.

Anand's subjectivism does not believe in drawing a self-portrait. He rearranges biographical elements and transforms them in a fiction in a way that they lose their personal meaning and become concrete human materials. The biographical approach obscures the proper comprehension of a literary process. E.M. Forster attaches greater importance to lower personality, which is inside the artist. The process of shifting from the conscious to the unconscious is a triumph for an artist. Anand's fiction is not an exception to this triumph. His autobiographical novels provide the background of the collective unconscious of India. Anand confesses in one of his interviews:

> The connection between my life and my writing is more intimate than in other novelists. I write as I live. My life is my message. (Rajan, 1986:95)

Anand's method of self-analysis in *The Bubble* accommodates a wide range of concerns and perceptions. Khushwant Singh in his review of the novel said,

> *The Bubble* may not be everybody's notion of a novel or an autobiography, but whatever it is, it is a great work. (34-35)

The Bubble, on final analysis, shows a greater sense and a profounder form of human existence. Krishan as the hero of the novel has been able to overcome his egocentric predicament because of the wider meaning through self-expiation and self-experience. His mind reaches beyond itself to assert an inter-relation with further reality. The self of Krishan asserts not only a spatio-temporal order but also a spiritual order of purpose, value and norm. He makes the actuality of our earthly life rich, full and wide. Krishan's quest for expansion and his zest for a vast world remind us of Aurobindo's observation:

> To know other countries is not to belittle but enlarge our own country and help it to a greater power of its being. (226)

We realize that Anand's excellence as an artist lies in the fact that he wrote his fiction for life's sake and not for art's sake. Art cannot be detached from life. All arts emerge from life and an artist, who portrays art devoid of life, is not an artist in the true sense. Art like poetry is a criticism of life. Art is rooted in life and it is mediation between the artist and the reality. Art that lures and conjures for sometimes and abjures at occasions is not art. An artist approaches life in a mood of high seriousness and absolute sincerity. Art contains a number of layers like life, fundamental temporality and timelessness. The surface variations of terrestrial life are as important as the hidden rhythms of universality in the fiction of Anand. Mulk Raj Anand is not only a crusader but also a creator of greater significance.

REFERENCES

Anand, Mulk Raj. *The Bubble*. New Delhi: Arnold Heinemann, 1984.

Aurobindo, Sri. *The Future Poetry*. Pondicherry: Arvind Ashram, 1972.

Brightman, Edgar Sheffield. "Personalistic Metaphysics of the Self: Its Distinctive Features" in *Radhakrishnan*, ed. W.R. Inge. London: Allen and Unwin, 1952.

Iyengar, K.R.S. *Indian Writing in English*. New Delhi: Sterling Publishers, 1987.

Maheshwari, V.K. *Preface* to *Perspectives on Indian English Literature*. New Delhi: Atlantic Publishers & Distributors, 2002.

Rajan, P.K. *Studies in Mulk Raj Anand*. New Delhi: Abhinav Prakashan, 1986.

Singh, Khushwant. 'A Delightful Autobiography' in the *Illustrated Weekly of India*. February 1985.

Mulk Raj Anand: A Messiah of Humanitarianism

9

Rahmat Jahan

The present world dominated by the culture of violence and terrorism has no use for humanitarianism, which it considers to be an outmoded creed. Of course, Prof. Amartya Sen was awarded Nobel Prize for 'welfare economics'. But his policy for welfare of the poors has few takers. Arundhati Roy, the great humanist gave away the amount of her Booker award to the downtrodden. In return, she was rewarded with a jail sentence for championing the cause of the millions uprooted from their natural habitat. Roy, piqued at this hypocrisy of the government, rejected the prestigious Sahitya Akademi award of 2005 in English literature for her book *The Algebra of Infinite Justice* in protest against the Indian government:

> ...violently and ruthlessly pursuing policies of brutalisation of industrial workers, increasing militarisation and economic neo-liberalisation. (*Hindustan Times*, 15 January 2006)

But humanitarianism is an essential part of human nature and will continue to survive till the existence of culture and civilisation. Humanitarianism is based upon the acceptance of compassion as a moral force and compassion is an undeniable fact of human consciousness inherent in human nature itself. This note of humanitarianism is struck in the writers of all ages. Cowper befriended 'Every animal that breathed'. Blake observed that, 'A Robin red breast in a cage/puts all Heaven in a rage.' Burns treated animals so intimately as if they belonged to his circle of friends. And Sterne desisted from hurting insects because, 'This world is wide enough to hold both thee and me.'

This humanitarian compassion included in its fold a wide range of unfortunate and unprivileged human beings who are fated to suffer at the hands of powerful forces. It includes the victims of an oppressive social order as in Dickens, the disgraced and the fallen or the mentally handicapped ones. In Hardy, man is pitted against Fate and Chance. Though being universal, this humanitarian ideal has gloriously flourished in the Indian culture. In Western culture, though compassion extends theoretically to both man and the animal kingdom, the *Bible* gives man dominion over the fish of the sea and over fowl of the air and every living thing that moved on the earth. In contrast, all animals, plants or that matter are taken to be manifestations of God in Indian culture. Hence, in Kalidasa's *Shakuntala*, the deer, the trees and the creepers weep when Shakuntala leaves the hermitage. In Western culture, compassion is only a value, but is a way of life in Indian thought. Lord Buddha and Lord Mahavira hence gave the first priority to *Karuna* (compassion) in his teachings. The Indian refrain '*Ahimsa Paramodharmah*' is too resonant to be overlooked. Mulk Raj Anand inheriting the legacy of both the Indian and Western thought claims to carry "the double burden on my shoulders, the Alps of the European tradition and the Himalaya of my Indian Past" (1975:67). Anand's circle of friends, according to Saros Cowasjee included writers like E.M. Forster, Herbert Read, Bonamy Dobree, T.S. Eliot, Aldous Huxley, Middleton Murray, Stephen Spender, Virginia Woolf, George Orwell, C. Day Lewis, Henry Miller, Dorothy Richardson and many others.

That his novels like *Untouchable* (1935) and *Coolie* (1936) have been translated in 38 languages of the world, testifies Anand's universal recognition and greatness. Most of his novels are inspired by his sympathy for the suffering, misery and helplessness of the unfortunate poors of the society at the hands of the capitalists or the feudal lords. As he himself claims in one of his letters to Saros Cowasjee, "Writing novels for the sake of writing novels was, as you know, never my intention. I felt compelled to answer challenges and tried to get out of my own confusion" (Anand, 1973:100). The inner experience of the protagonist is very vividly portrayed in the long reverie sequence of Bakha in *Untouchable* after he has been slapped on the face by a high caste man. This has been attributed very convincingly to the effect of stream of consciousness technique employed by James Joyce in *Ulysses*.

Untouchable, Anand's very first novel, inaugurates the literature of the downtrodden. It was indeed a revolutionary gesture in Indian fiction to choose an untouchable as hero in 1935. Equally significant is the fact that Bakha, the hero of *Untouchable,* was a latrine cleaner belonging to the lowest rung of the hierarchy within the class of untouchables. Bakha strikes as an authentic rather than a romantic low class hero because Anand as a boy had actually played with untouchable boys, when his father was working in a regiment, to which a sweeper colony was attached. E.M. Forster in this regard had said:

> *Untouchable* could only have been written by an Indian, and by an Indian who observed from the outside. No European, however sympathetic, could have created the character, because he would not have known enough about his troubles. And no untouchable could have written the book, because he would have been involved in indignation and self pity. (1984, vi)

Bakha is humiliated, cursed and bullied. He is compelled to announce his approach by crying 'Posh, posh, sweeper is coming', lest he may defile the twice born Brahmins like Pandit Kali Nath. Cigarettes are flung at him as a bone is flung at an insistent sniffing dog, jalebis are thrown at him like waste thrown at a pig and the thin paperlike pancake flies down to him like a kite from the third floor. He has to bear the brunt of his caste as such:

> Get off the step scavenger? Off with you? You have defiled our temple! Now you will have to pay for the purification. Get down, get away, dog! (1984:69)

'Bakha,' says E.M. Forster, "is a real individual, lovable, thwarted, sometimes grand, sometimes weak, and thoroughly Indian." Above all, he has to suffer the humiliation of finding his sister being molested by a lascivious priest.

Anand, but, is fully aware of the fact that objectivity is vitally important in a novel of protest. Bakha's entire day is interspersed with linings of joy too. After a wicked woman scolds and drives away Bakha from the wooden platform outside her house, a kind woman consoles him by giving him a chapati and gently advising him "My child you should not sit on people's doorsteps like this." Havildar Charat Singh too seems to be very liberal and allows Bakha in his kitchen and he even pours tea from his own tumbler into the pan in Bakha's hand. The day brings Bakha two great gifts, a brand new hockey stick, the present from the generous Havildar Charat Singh and secondly the gift of hope that someday he will be redeemed. Characterwise also, there is no division between absolute black and white. The untouchables in the novel are not all angels, nor are the upper caste men all devils. Bakha, unlike the common untouchable looks intelligent, sensitive and dignified. Whereas his brother is described wearing:

> tattered flannel shirt, grimy with the blowings of his ever running nose, obstructed his walk slightly. Flies congregated in abundance...on his dirty face...to taste the sweet delights of the saliva on the corners of his lips.

Anand, the novelist par excellence, does not allow his humanitarianism to override the formal values of the narrative. The narrative shows three clear stages of development, all during a single day. Each stage presents an intermingling of pleasant and unpleasant experiences. Bakha's day begins with his father's scoldings and the rigorous morning tasks but he looks forward to getting the gift of a hockey stick later in the day. He is merrily moving through the market place with a packet of *jalebis* but all of a sudden his collision with a caste Hindu shatters all his joy. This first stage occupies less than one third of the novel. The second stage occupying about half of the book also comprises several meaningful incidents. There is the shocking incident of the sexual assault of Bakha's sister Rohini by a priest compensated by the triumph of Bakha's scoring a goal with his new hockey stick. Again he gets a brushing from his father which upsets his mood. This stage occupies slightly less than half of the book. Anand, at the end of the novel, rules out any possibility of being bracketed as a social reformer. Three possible solutions to his problem are suggested to Bakha: one, 'Conversion to Christianity', secondly 'the acceptance of the Flush System' and finally, 'Abolition of untouchability'. But he is not shown accepting any particular solution to his problem.

Just like *Untouchable*'s Bakha is inspired by Anand's childhood friendship with a sweeper boy, *Coolie*'s protagonist Munoo is based on his intimacy with his childhood playmate. Munoo's suffering as a labourer in a pickle factory and his helplessness in this perspective forms the leit-motif of *Coolie*. V.S. Pritchett (2000:53):

> ...got more out of *Coolie* than out of any other novel I have read for a very long time indeed. There is so much talk about political novels in these times but so few of them seem to me to be works of any high order. In fact *Coolie* is the only political novel I have read which profoundly satisfied me.

When Munoo gets engaged in fetching water for the elephant in circus, the elephant trainer cautions him:

> The bigger a city is, the more cruel it is to the sons of Adam.... You have to pay even for the breath you breathe. (1985:177)

Munoo comes to realise that there are only two kinds of people in the world: the rich and the poor, and between the two there is no connection. The magnificence and glory of the rich thrives on the misery and helplessness of the poor. According to Saros Cowasjee, it is Munoo's innocence which weaves the magic of the book. He is the Indian counterpart of Charles Dicken's *David Copperfield* and is precisely speaking, the voice of the misery of India. "If *Untouchable* is a microcosm, *Coolie* is a macrocosm, that is Indian society", (265) says K.R. Srinivas Iyengar. It is a story of a country in the throes of capitalism and religious fanaticism, the sweetest song of the coolies that tell of their saddest thoughts with the chorus: "We belong to suffering! We belong to suffering! my love" (1985:247).

Munoo is an orphan village boy from the Kangra hills. He works in turns as a domestic servant in an urban middle class family, as a labourer in a Bombay cotton mill and as a rickshaw puller in Shimla. His life account very effectively delineates the exploitation of the poor by rich and powerful. The picture here again is very realistically balanced. Ill treated and underfed most of the time, Munoo also enjoys the filial affection of a gentle employer. Munoo's life is not a complete saga of dark sorrow. He is comforted and attended by an Anglo Indian nurse when he is seriously ill. It is this sense of balance that saves humanitarian motif from the pitfalls of tearful sentimentality.

The theme of exploitation is more poignantly presented in *Two Leaves and a Bud* (1937) with a tea plantation as background. It deals with two different sections; the British officials and their subordinates on one hand representing the exploiter group and the helpless coolies on the other hand comprising the group of the exploited. It launches an aggressive attack on the inhuman capitalist economy, harmful effects of imperialism and the subsequent exploitation and harassment of helpless labourers. Gangu is the protagonist whose imploring for a loan to cremate his wife fall on deaf ears:

> Can you give a loan of money for the cremation? I have not a piece and the body has been lying in the house for two days. (1983:118)

Even the Doctor Sahib, John de la Havre who pleads on behalf of the labourers has to face the ire of the British official Reggie Hunt:

> Let de la Havre mind his own business. Back you go, swine, back you go to the lines.... (206)

To John de la Havre, a cup of tea is nothing but "The hunger, the sweat and the despair of a million Indians." Gangu, in turn, is perplexed by this high-handedness and quizzes:

> Did all the sahibs who come to own this land get their labourers by letting lies pass for truth, did they make deceit a virtue and exalt the worst to the best, make every pushful duffer like Buta into a sardar and liberate all the selfishness that any charlatan could use for his

> own purpose ? Do all good men die here, and others live on? (65)

As per the incidents and the casting of the novel, John de la Havre, Miss Barbara and Narain, the coolie, seem to be the mouthpieces of Anand, the novelist, through whom he is voicing his social criticism of the evils of capitalism.

Gauri (1960) one of the finest novels of Anand affords an insight into the mind and heart of a rustic woman. It also depicts how she undergoes epic transformation in her character, personality and fortune over the years. Born in a typical Indian family, she after marriage tries to resign to her lot. *Gauri* eloquently exposes the hypocrisy of the decrepit Indian society which treats a woman as a commodity devoid of any personal identity:

> Panchi in *Gauri* proceeds elatedly on an unwilling pony to possess the girl whom he could fold in his arms at night and kick during the day, who would adorn his house and help him with the land. (1984:11)

The shrewd and cruel aunt-in-law and suspicious husband conspire to drive her out of the house. Gauri, when driven out of the husband's house returns to her mother's house where also she is not at all welcome. Returning to her husband's house once again, she faces the same fate. Her aunt-in-law Kesaro continues her hate campaign against her calling her "a whore from Piplan", "a filthy woman", "sweeper woman shameless". Time and again Panchi heaps the choicest invectives on Gauri casting doubts on her fidelity. The devil in him yells:

> Tell me the truth bitch.... What is the proof of your purity? (262)

Panchi even in the most passionate moment reminds Gauri of his conventional right to beat her:

> But the husband has to chastise wife if she goes wrong, he said airily. So says, our Dharam. (51)

But Gauri is mature enough not to be so gullible as to pray to the earth to swallow her up like her legendary counterpart. She, instead, takes up the job of a nurse in a city hospital. The rustic, mute, passive Gauri of the opening of the novel is transformed into a bold, self-confident and self-reliant woman.

Mulk Raj Anand is pained by the apathy of Indian society which accords woman the status of a slave "bound and fecund to the service of the hearth...." Rukmani in Anand's *The Road* (1961), whose marriage was delayed for want of money to give dowry, is puzzled at this arrogance of males and asks:

> Oh why, why were the men of tribe so privileged? (1961:100)

Social taboos, believed Anand, cannot be broken with mere law making; the entire mindset of male chauvinism has to be overhauled. It was with this motive that he wrote novels like *Gauri* to make people realise the ill-treatment meted out to women, the harbinger of new generation. It is his most successful endeavour towards the emancipation of women. The novel, as the author rightly tells us, is his "offering to the beauty, dignity and devotion of Indian women".

Anand's novels have evoked appreciations galore from scholars far and wide. E.M. Forster who also wrote the preface of *Untouchable* calls it:

> ...an excellent work and I am delighted it is being reprinted. I hope it will be again favourably received (Anand, 1984).

For K.R. Srinivas Iyengar, an authority on Indian English literature,

> Anand's notable marks are vitality and a keen sense of actuality. He is a veritable Dickens for describing the inequities and idiosyncrasies in the current human situation with candour as well as accuracy. (130)

His most ambitious project, however, happens to be an autobiographical novel in seven volumes entitled *Seven Ages of Man*. It is modelled on Shakespeare's poem 'All the World's a Stage' which occurs in his comedy *As You Like It*. Anand has till now completed only four volumes of *Seven Ages of Man*. The first volume entitled *Seven Summers* spans the first seven years of the hero Krishan Chander's life which, in actuality, recapitulates Anand's own childhood. The second volume *Morning Face* (1968) deals with only six years in the hero Krishan's life from the beginning of World War I to the Jallianwala Bagh Massacre. In 1976 was published the third volume *Confessions of a Lover* which deals with Krishan Chander's life at Khalsa College from 1921 to 1924. In due course it explores Anand's multifarious loves: his love of political and social freedom, his love of the Mahatma, his love of verse, and above all his love for his beloved Yasmin.

Published in 1984 was the fourth volume *The Bubble.* Complete in ten parts, it encompasses letters, diaries and journals. It also covers Krishan's years abroad from 1925 to 1929 and its primary focus is on Anand's emotional encounter with Irene Rhys. Irene leaves Anand to participate in her country Ireland's struggle for independence. It is this commitment of Irene for her country which kindles the fire of patriotism in the young Anand. *And So He Plays His Part*, the fifth volume of his epic is being worked upon by Anand since the last few years. This novel with seven parts depicts his conversion from a Western scholar to a typically Indian writer. It is with great eagerness that scholars were waiting for the publication of the sixth and seventh volume of this autobiographical novel which he intended to title as *As World Too Wide* and *Last Scene*. But destiny willed otherwise and this venture of Anand has been cut short as fate stole his existence from the physical world on 28-9-2004.

To Anand are also attributed half a dozen short story collections. And these are animated by a distinct theme of humanitarianism. The prolific novelist shows a rare skill in delving into the minds of a dove, peacock and chicks. *The Lost Child*, undoubtedly one of the finest short stories of Indian language, deftly explores the child psychology and adult psychology simultaneously. Anand's more than twenty-five novels and collections of short stories throbbing with humanitarianism are torch bearers for the humanity to develop understanding and compassion, sympathy and fellow feeling. They deserve to be studied for a catholicity of outlook, deep human warmth, an insight into the human heart and nearness to life.

REFERENCES

Anand, Mulk Raj. *The Road*. Bombay: Kutub-Popular, 1961.

——. *Apology for Heroism*, New Delhi: Arnold Heinemann, 1975.

——. *Two Leaves and a Bud*. New Delhi: Arnold Heinemann, 1983.

——. *Gauri*. New Delhi: Arnold Heinemann, 1984.

——. *Untouchable*. New Delhi: Arnold Heinemann, 1984.

——. *Coolie*. New Delhi: Arnold Heinemann, 1985.

Cowasjee, Saros, Ed. *Author to Critic—The Letters of Mulk Raj Anand to Saros Cowasjee*. Calcutta: Writers Workshop, 1973.

Hindustan Times, January 15, 2006.

Iyengar, K.R. Srinivasa. *Indian Writing in English*. Bombay: Asia Publishing House, 1973.

Pritchett, V.S. in George, C.J. *Mulk Raj Anand: His Art and Concerns*. New Delhi: Atlantic Publishers and Distributors, 2000.

Mulk Raj Anand in Letters

10

R.C.P. Yadav

To have a right access to and a real grasp of what Anand wrote in the form of novels and short stories one needs to go through his letters addressed to his friends and scholars working on him and to his contemporaries known as Indians and the world class creative personalities of the western hemisphere of the globe.

So, it was to understand Anand's writings adequately that I planned a regular correspondence with him as a research scholar or what this avant-garde of literature brands as 'a thesis writer'. Before I plunged myself into writing something meaningful on him, I wanted to write to him with a long list of my questionnaire on the subject of my thesis. Since the subject of my thesis was the entire corpus of his fiction, there was a number of questions to be answered by him partly for my personal 'pleasure and edification' and partly for my pretentious claim to the height of fame as an authority on this young—old artist who matters most to millions of have-nots even after he is not physically with them any more.

But this ambitious plan was not to be materialised unless I was introduced to him by one of his acquaintances or dared to see him at his Bombay residence or at his Khandala Palace amidst nature without any letter of introduction by any one he knew closely.

I seized upon an opportunity to look into the pages of a book on Anand by an Emeritus Professor Dr. M.K. Naik of Dharwar University, Karnataka. I wrote to him straightway asking for Anand's address for contact. He very kindly responded to my letter and gave me all I needed for my correspondence with this great living literary legend.

Professor Naik's bounty filled me with an unyielding sense of courage and confidence to go on in my literary pursuit, and out of my hunches for making Anand my friend, philosopher and guide, I, at once, wrote to him on his Cuffe Parade address praying for his valuable suggestion regarding the selection of the burden of my research project. Without an iota of inhibition he wrote back to me with an unfailing sense of co-operation in my literary venture, saying in words like:

> The area which has not been covered is the ethos from the early novels till today. The emergence of the characters from existentialism to the awareness of human predicament in the sense in which the characters want to become heroes. And though they fail, they struggle. This can only be brought out, if the thesis deals with protest elements in my novels and stories. (January 13, 1978)

Elated at the expressions used by Anand in his first letter, I wanted to concentrate on 'the ethos' of his novel, and on the awareness of his characters of human predicament. And my attempt was to hunt for this element of protest in his fiction.

In quick succession I dropped another letter requesting him to give me some more light on my research riddles, but this letter of mine remained unacknowledged for some time, as Dr. Anand had been away on a Marg research tour. Sometime later in a humorous vein he explained his position and his inability to answer letters timely:

> I am at least useful for my countrymen as a joke—a pompous ass who pretends to do wonderful things, but can't answer letters. (April 20, 1978)
>
> As for 'ethos' he wanted me to go through his books as they themselves 'may reveal bits & pieces of insight'. (April 20, 1978)

Any dependence on Indian critics would hardly help me in having a multi-or-mega dimensional image of Anand as they 'seem to have partial views true to the legend about the Blind man and the Elephant' (April 20, 1978).

Anand was all admiration for European critics like Jack Lindsay, Reimenschneider, Alastair Niven and India born Saros Cowasjee for the simple reason that 'they seem to have grasped the overall trend of sympathy from which the novels were written' (April 20, 1978).

All was not well with Anand when he heard that all the books published in India after *Private Life* had been dismissed by one of the Indian critics. He reacted vehemently to such prejudice and pettiness in the following words:

> It would be invidious for me to say anything to me, because he is a Brown Sahib of the latest brand of snobs, who will descend to pettiness to defend himself. (June 22, 1978)
>
> Deeply wounded by the unjust and unseemly comments passed by the latest brand of snobs, he expressed the hope that 'here and there away from orthodox critics, I may be understood. (August 02, 1978)

He took no notice of his compatriots and he condoned their bad education knowing it full well that they often did not know what they were saying:

> Look at the abuse hurled on Tagore by his own compatriots in Bengal before he won world recognition. Sharat Babu was equally abused. Prem Chand still remains a provincial figure, because none of the critics were ever able to recognize his importance all these years, until UNESCO published *Godan*. (April 26, 1979)

Shifting from pettiness to the discussion of some palatable points of Anand's craft of fiction, his attention was drawn to answer the question about how the novel *Untouchable* did stop short of Col. Hutchinson, the Mahatma and the poet. His answer was:

> It would not have been a novel then, but reportage. The novel, as I understand it, requires formal construction, giving a total view of life rather than fragmented bits of

> consciousness of the hero. As you are doubtless aware, in our country, the outcastes live under the shadow of white livered humanitarians, the Mahatma and pseudo intellectuals, who don't enter into the consciousness of the folk twice, but are dimly apprehended. Without them in the total picture this novel would have remained a slice of life and not strong enough to suggest the vision of possible change. (July 12, 1978)

To my significant question what did he mean by protest in his novel, he expressed his answer analytically in the following words:

> When I say protest in a novel, I mean the up rush of feeling, not the imposition of thought; a conversion does not happen from a sermon, but from some odd compulsion in one's emotional life. (July 12, 1978)

This inner fabric of protest could be felt in novels like *Untouchable*, *Coolie, Two Leaves and a Bud* and many others. Through these works Anand attempted to plead for those who were the 'flesh of his flesh and the blood of his blood':

> I tried with all my heart and mind to recreate some of the human beings of my time, so that the world should know those who had no mouths to utter anything about their anguish.... (April 26, 1979)

As for another pertinent question if his novel had any traditional plot. His pointblank answer was:

> The narrative here is supposed to hang together from the relation of one character to the other, so there is no need for a story or a plot—inner causalities link the novella. I do not believe in any plot. (August 02, 1978)

Many more letters of patriarchal nature that I continued to receive till the completion of my research schedule, remind me of *Nehru's Letters to His Daughter*.

All these letters, as I understand, would be considered as a piece of literature. They have influenced me in such great measure that I can say safely that I knew clearly what protest literature is, from these letters. When my book *The Body-Soul*

Drama was published, I sent a copy of this book for his reaction. On receiving the book he took no time in sending his reaction by airmail. I can never forget his words of encouragement for me:

> Thank you for the book *The Body-Soul Drama* that you have written about the inner core of my writings. You are one of the few critics who is seized upon the interior motivations. (July 14, 1999)

In referring these unpublished letters to the readers my intention is to show that they will go a long way to understand fully Anand the man and Anand the creative artist committed emotionally to the cause of the depraved and the dispossessed like Bakha, Munoo, Gangu, Lal Singh, Ananta, Gauri, Bhikhu, Nur, Maqbool Sherwani and Krishan Chander 'Azad'. They struggle against social injustice heaped on them by the property owning class. They want to come up for air out of the lower depth created by the rich.

Lastly these letters, serving as literary weapons, would help one to be bold enough to plead from the housetops that:

> Mulk Raj Anand is a committed artist. His novels are not without political overtones. But his art lies in suggesting those ideals by implication. And it is the implication that signifies in a work of art. His fiction besides being a work of art is protest literature not devoid of high imaginative awareness and mature technique. (Yadav, 1998:150)

REFERENCES

M.R. Anand's letters to the author:

Letter, January 13, 1978.

——, April 20, 1978.

——, June 22, 1978.

——, July 12, 1978.

——, August 2, 1978.

——, April 26, 1979.

——, July 14, 1999.

Yadav, R.C.P. *The Body-Soul Drama*. Purnea; Delhi: Rachanakar Prakashan, 1998.

Anand's *Seven Summers*—An Analytical Study

11

Raihan Raza

The publisher's blurb to *Morning Face* describes *Seven Summers* as "the first part of a seven volume long novel, *Seven Ages of Man*, a source book of the novels and stories of Mulk Raj Anand". Both the title 'Seven Summers' and the subtitle 'The Story of an Indian Childhood' indicate the scope and nature of the volume. The mood of the novel is indicated by the epigraph used by Anand:

> I love roads, I love lanes and streets: I love walk, walk, walk, for it is an opportunity for thought developing into a clear process, often leading to self-illumination and discovery, thanks to the sound of one's own foot falls.... (1960)

Of the seven volumes of *Seven Ages of Man*, only four volumes, *Seven Summers, Morning Face, Confession of a Lover* and *The Bubble* have appeared. Anand believed in the confessional novel, as is clear from: "I believe in the confessional novel. In the first person singular, one can be nearly honest, peel the onion layer by layer, get to one's conscience" (1972:33). Anand in his *Seven Ages of Man* uses the technique of the first person singular. In *Seven Summers* Krishan Chander, the narrator hero of the novel recollects the experiences of his own childhood, which are not different from Anand's own early life. The child-hero, like his creator, struggles for various freedoms as he grows in years. Anand writes: "I adopted Krishan Chander as the name of the fictional hero of my autobiographical novel, because a new Krishna seemed to be called for. And the "I" of the narrator had to be distinguished from the character Krishan Chander, who is also me, to a large extent" (Cowasjee,

1977:168). It is further interesting to note that in his 'Dedication' to *Morning Face* Anand indicated some possible approaches to the character of his protagonist in *Seven Summers* and *Morning Face*. Addressing Krishan Chander, he said: "When you first appeared in *Seven Summers*, the critics said variously that you were an incarnation of Krishna of the Yadus or just a Panjabi 'spark'. They were not far wrong, because, if I may confess to you the truth, the old myth was dormant in my heart and mind as these myths are inherited by every Indian.... The 'spark' of the street urchin was, however, also in me and I may have imbued you with it. But...you are really not the Krishna of the age of gods. You cannot be, because the age of the gods is over, you seem to be aspiring to the new contemporary myth of man of the *Kaliyug*, the iron age, in which Money itself, as a vast impersonal mechanism of power, inexorably governs life, like an unknown Fate, as the unknown Gods, or the unknown evil in man, commanded life in the past, pursuing its seemingly mysterious ends, indifferent to the feelings of men and women" (1968:v).

It is outside the scope of the present investigation to go into the merits of the four published volumes of *Seven Ages of Man* as autobiographical novels. But superficially it appears that they are autobiographies with fictional overtones. In *Seven Summers*, Anand shows the influence of Tolstoy's *Childhood*, a work which is not strictly speaking autobiographical. Like him, Anand has a remarkable capacity for wonder that allows him to present his childhood from a child's viewpoint. Krishan rightly grows lyrical in the novel about the state of childhood:

> Childhood, oh childhood! How easy it is for one to yield to the slightest happiness and the merest breath of sorrow in one's childhood! And is there any joy as pure or any sorrow as fleeting as that of childhood? What was the magic of those days, which is not here today? ...Was it the innocence of one's soul or the sheer vitality of one's body? (34)

Seven Summers is divided into two parts: 'The Road' and 'The River'. Both these subtitles are symbolic of the hero's development. "The road and the river are associated with time and acquisition of knowledge. Both symbols register the passing of general human time, and each represents a stage in Krishna's development and widening knowledge of the world—'The Road' section his first five years and 'The River' section the remaining years of childhood. The child's development, which begins as an impression of reality, proceeds to questions about the nature of that reality" (Harrex, 1977:131). The novel begins when the hero is three years old. He is fascinated by the road, though his mother has asked him not to cross it:

> Dividing the barracks and the bungalows is the road, lined with casuarina trees, which stretches from end to end of the horizon. I stand for a long while with my thumb in my mouth wondering where it comes from and where it goes. Then I run round in circles on the little clearing under the grove surrounding the Persian wheel well in a wild delirium of movement, oblivious of the past and the future, excited by my own happiness at finding myself wandering freely in the wide open world.... (7)

This road of the cantonment of Mian Mir where Krishan's father is a respectable Head Clerk in the army is the starting point of the journey of his life. It is a symbol of his initiation into life. "The road obviously symbolizes the journey of life, but it symbolizes some thing else besides: it is the road that divides the rich from the poor, the barracks of the sepoys from the plush bungalows of the white officers. To a child yet untouched by the world's sorrows, the road stretches 'from end to end of the horizon'. He will in the course of time travel it, but for the present he must follow his mother's injunctions and not cross it" (Cowasjee, 1977:168). Soon Krishan crosses the road out of the spirit of enquiry and zest for life:

> ...the road which I crossed from the protection of one line of casuarina trees, stirred by the nimble breeze, to the other, the road in whose dust I rolled, the road where I held conversation with men and beasts and birds, the road which dominated my life with its unknown past and its undiscovered future. (27-28)

The road's rhythm becomes Krishan's rhythm:

> ...as though the road were in me and the whole world all about me, stretching for miles and miles and miles into nebulous lands uncharted by my mind.... The forefinger of amazement was in my mouth as I stood there.... (57)

Krishan is nicknamed Bully the Budmash and he lives up to his reputation. The passing away of Prithvi, his younger brother, leaves him sad. The bear dance, however, reduces his sorrow. The spirit of enquiry is soon awakened in him and he pesters his parents with many innocent questions such as the following:

> 'Where did you find me, mother?'
> 'Where did I come from ?'...
> 'Who made God, mother ?' (58)

The feeling of rebellion is also born when he is beaten by his father for stealing a mango. It:

> ...largely transformed me into an uncompromising rebel that I became, gave the spoilt, self-willed child in me the impetus of an overdeveloped sense of grievance and misery.... There sprang perhaps from this ridiculous incident the lava of violence in me which sizzled like an active volcano during my boyhood, till my whole life become a series of constant eruptions. (140)

Krishan continues his adventures. He mixes with the sepoys and untouchables despite his mother's instructions to the contrary. Lakha's son, Bakha, is his friend. Ram Charan, Ali, Chotta and most of his other friends are also poor. Bakha appears as:

> a black colossus with his enormous turban unstuck and his thick khaki tunic and shorts sodden with sweat and dirt. (137)

Krishan recalls his days with Bakha and others:

> How much kinder and more prodigal in their generosity were these humble, poor sepoys, workmen and untouchables than my own parents who regarded themselves as their superiors and always forbade me to

> touch anything belonging to them. Certainly, I learnt a great deal of what I know now from these people, the gift for making things, of telling a tale..., and all my manhood was built upon the experiences of these irrelevant moments spent in truancy. (169-70)

It is such characters and events that Krishan refers to that figure again in his early novels lifted from Krishan's childhood. "...*Seven Summers* does have some specific affinities with the early novels, particularly *Untouchable*. Bakha, Chotta (sic) and Ram Charan in *Untouchable* grew out of the early draft of *Seven Summers* and there are also duplications of incidents" (Harrex, 1977:128). The spirit of enquiry and the zest for life, which are among the salient features of the young hero, increase when the family shifts to Nowshera cantonment. Here too he pesters his mother with his 'whys' and 'wherefores'. The casual reply that his godmother is in *Vilayat* keeps him obsessed with the longing for going abroad. Then he is sent to school, which he soon finds out, is a prison with the teacher as the jailor, a veritable taskmaster and a terror to the boys, with his cane ever ready to 'educate' them.

The 'road' section of the novel explains the individual's connection with society. Krishan grows up and while he grows up, he is fully initiated into life. He views his parents, with a mixed feeling of affection, curiosity, and anger. An important feature of Krishan in the process of developing is his attraction for women. Besides his mother and aunts, he is attracted towards young girls, and their very touch gives him sensual pleasure. When lacking company, he would imagine a female playmate and speak to her aloud. "He (Krishan—Anand) is as Freudian a baby as was ever born in English fiction of the twenties and the thirties (the birth-rate seems to have fallen since), and his seven summers are hot with his physical love for his mother and aunts" (Cowasjee, 1977:169).

Among other memorable events of Krishan Chander's childhood days is his visit with his father to Delhi where he gets lost for a while. Meanwhile, he goes with his mother to Daska where he gets the first glimpses of lovely and serene country life from which he returns perforce to Nowshera owing to a quarrel between his mother and aunt. Krishan is revealed as an inquisitive boy with wide-open eyes, ever ready to receive all sorts of impressions he comes by.

Although *Seven Summers* is an account of Krishan's childhood strictly from a child's viewpoint, it has plenty of details about the joint family, arranged marriages, adult differences of opinion, the younger generation's striving for independence, domestic and conventional ritual, etc. "The novel is significant both as an authentic document of the childhood days of Anand, now a recognized international intellectual force, and also as an imaginative reconstruction of the social, economic, and political life of India at the beginning of this century" (Gupta, 1974:104-05). The sociological aspects of Indian life are highlighted by Krishan Chander's growing consciousness. The way Harish and Draupadi are pushed together in marriage has been typical of the attitude of parents to marriage in India, at least till recently. Most of these marriages are arranged by parents—seldom in consultation with the girl, partly on astrological considerations and partly on the considerations of the prestige of the two families, and, of course, dowry. Consequently, the young ones are often forced to suffer maladjustment and unhappiness. The sociological realities, however, are presented through a child's impressions. "Innocence, bubbling joy and instinctive life underline this delicate and touching story, and laughter rings through its pages. Characters remain permanently etched in our minds, and sweet nothings of day-to-day life suddenly reveal their meaning and their significance, humor and farce are as common in the story as they are in actual childhood. Ali, with his running nose, the strange fakir giving a realistic demonstration of rifle practice with a dummy rifle to collect alms from the sepoys, the school master Din Gul and his severe punishment—all ring through the portals of his memory and become alive under the white heat of his imagination. *Seven Summers* is the most important book in the field of child-literature" (Mehta, 1979:178). It is largely true that the inner world of the child-hero and the outer one of the society in which he lives and grows are integrated together by Krishan's child-consciousness but as he grows up he gradually sheds his innocence. It, however, has made the novel a compact narrative.

The broad features of Krishan's childhood correspond to Anand's life. The vivid realism and intensity with which he has described them proves that they are all outstanding events of his childhood. But the novel suffers at places when he allows his adult consciousness to interfere with his recreation of his early childhood. The two passages quoted below illustrate the observation:

> In the light of those days I am now inclined to think that childhood is not altogether the happy golden time sentimentalists make it out to be as a compensation for the rigours of the grown-up world, but that it is characterized by long patches of loneliness when children are condemned, for good or ill, to the prisons of their own devices if there is not available a crèche or a kindergarten or swing and the company of other children. It is true that the lonely child develops an almost convalescent sensitiveness under these circumstances and creates fantasies for his own delectation, but the burden of this early effort, though profitable in the long run, is heavy to bear when the tender soul has constantly to jump from the dreamy existence of the garden bower to the world of reality which is made up of the parental routine of meals and siestas. (27)

> A great deal of this abject misery is due to the lack of understanding of children by the elders who have forgotten their own childhood and ignore the young or apply standards derived from their own peculiar adult experience, mixed with pompous notions of what is good for those who are growing up. (218-19)

Such examples are, however, occasional and do not detract readers from the merit of *Seven Summers* as an autobiography of childhood. "The mature Anand can be seen leaning over the shoulders of the young hero and guiding him in his narration, but he does it so subtly and with such restraint that his presence is not obtrusive. The story remains consistent with the child's point of view" (Cowasjee, 1977:174). It is not surprising that *Seven Summers* is "the best autobiography of childhood yet written by an Indian novelist in English" (175).

Being an autobiographical work with a confessional strain, *Seven Summers* is of special value as an aid to our understanding of Anand's fiction. As already stated, Anand believes in the confessional novel. Although he employs this form, his use is different from that of Proust or Sylvia Plath. *Seven Summers* gives an insight into the various incidents, which impinged on the consciousness of Anand as a boy, and any study that is involved in tracing the influences on Anand the writer, benefits greatly from a study of *Seven Summers*. One might go so far as to assert that the distinctive voice of his fiction owes much to his early life. "That Anand started imbibing humanist faith right from his childhood becomes amply evident from *Seven Ages of Man*. The hero being Anand himself, we see how he gradually developed certain convictions, which actually form the different tenets of Anand's humanism. Anand's abhorrence of superstition and fatalism, poverty and cruelty, his denunciation of God and religiosity, imperialism and imperfect education, his plea for liberty and compassion, his defense of women's rights, and lastly, his advocacy of the cause of the lowly and the lost-all. These humanist ideas are shown as points of faith which Anand, or the hero of *Seven Ages of Man*, develops as a result of his actual experiences in life" (Gupta, 1974:104).

From Anand's early fiction it appears that he knows his characters personality. For his material he draws largely on his personal experiences. He is aware that "the author must know his people, be as familiar with them as though the men were his constant tavern companions, the women his loving doxies and the children his own brats" (Fox, 1956:167). Regarding his fictional characters, Anand has said: "All these heroes, as the other men and women who had emerged in my novels and short stories, were reflections of the real people I had known during my childhood and youth. And I was only repaying the debt of gratitude I owed them for much of the inspiration they had given me to mature manhood, when I began to interpret their lives in my writing. They were not mere phantoms.... They were flesh of my flesh and blood of my blood, and obsessed me in the way in which certain human beings obsess an artist's soul. And I was doing no more than what a writer does when he seeks to interpret the truth from the realities of his life" (Anand, 1951). This is true of most of his heroes like Bakha, Munoo, Gangu, Nihal Singh and Ananta. *Seven Summers* shows how Bakha, the hero of *Untouchable*, is a figure from Anand's childhood. In this novel Bakha appears as

> "a black colossus with his enormous turban unstuck and his thick khaki tunic and shorts sodden with sweat and dirt". (137)

Krishan is shown playing with him in the playground without the least sense of pollution complex. Lakha, Bakha's father, and many of his companions such as Chota, Ram Charan, Ali and Abdulla figure in both *Seven Summers* and *Untouchable*. Similarly, many incidents figuring in *Untouchable* are lifted from Anand's childhood as presented in *Seven Summers*. The incident in *Untouchable* where Bakha picks up a small boy hurt by a flying stone in the melee over the hockey match and is abused by the boy's mother is lifted with minor changes from *Seven Summers*.

Although Krishan's mother asks him not to associate with the untouchables, he plays with them, and the emotional sympathy and humanistic attitude with which Anand has portrayed Bakha, Munoo and Gangu are derived from his childhood days. The influence of Gandhi did give an intellectual edge to his love for the poor and the downtrodden but it was already ingrained in the novelist.

Education is a major theme in *Seven Summers*. When Krishan is sent to school, he soon finds out that it is a prison with the teacher as the jailor, and canes the only language of educating children. Anand provides in this novel a few glimpses of his primary school life. His first impressions of school are recorded in this novel:

> A sudden terror gripped me as I stood in the tense silence of the room watching the boys being beaten. (97-98)

With teachers like Din Gul and Trilok Chand who believed that the only effective way of imparting any instruction was through slapping and caning boys, and filling the classroom with tears, sobs and howls, it is nothing short of terror:

> After the few times I had been flogged at school a sense of doom had taken possession of me, creeping into my skin, till the whirring of the cane in my imagination was enough to start tears in my eyes. (141)

This type of schooling had a specific object. Krishan tells how his own father, like most others of his generation, thought of education in terms of mere degrees, which would make men babus with some safe job in government service. In his non-fiction Anand has severely criticized the type of education he received: "What is the education...we do want for our children? The answer is that we want the kind of education which releases their potential creative energies, which does not impose anything on them that they do not want but which liberates them instead, which demands little from them but gives them much, which is not taking it out of the children to appease our own frustration, but which is giving without an ulterior motive to the extent to which it is humanly possible to give...such an education is built on our real love of the children and not on false love which is hatred...such an education does not consist of adult moralizing and the exercise of an authority which is mostly the rationalization of our self-complacent belief in our own importance and from the point of view of which we think children good or bad as long as they fulfill our adult standards of respectable behavior.... Suppression and repression and cane-driven sense are not education at all" (Anand, 1949:176-77).

The criticism of the type of schooling and education that Krishan/Anand and the children of his generation received in British Indian schools is presented in Anand's novel, *Lament on the Death of a Master of Arts* (1938). Nur, the hero of the novel, recalls his past. He remembers how cruel and revengeful was his teacher who had once savagely beaten him up with a cane. The punishment he received for a mere slip in spelling is incredibly cruel: "...the Master was putting pencils between his fingers and pressing them hard, hard, harder, and Nur could see himself writhing and shrieking and crying as he rolled on the floor to release his cracking bones from the Master's grasp..." (1939:37-38). Like Krishan, Nur is filled with terror at the vision of his school. Through the past and the present plight of Nur, Anand shows how modern education leaves one misfit. The desire of Nur's father that Nur should become a collector makes Nur's life miserable. He is unable to fulfill the ambition of his father. It would have been better for Nur, if he had followed his father's profession and become a confectioner. Nur's example exemplifies the frustration that follows such education. The novelist's treatment of this theme is backed by his experiences: "The education I received at school and college was a spurious, imitative, fruitless grounding, mainly through a foreign language, in useless bits of history, geography, mathematics and the elements of science. I got not an iota of knowledge of India's past culture through all this schooling, and very little genuine appreciation of European culture...there was no connection between the learning imparted to me and the actual world, in which, apart from a few snobbish, rich and prosperous people, everyone was frustrated, tormented and restless, and continually weeping over his suffering" (1949:3).

It is in instances of this nature that Anand finds his early impressions as viable data for critical evaluation. The impressions themselves—the callousness, the indignity, the humiliation of it all—persist in the mind and in *Confessions*, and subsequently in *Seven Summers* they appear undimmed in intensity and detail, because during the intervening years they had transmitted new experience into thought which became, so to speak, the 'objective correlative' of the sordid emotions felt in childhood, and recreated in Anand's fiction with a purity of feeling that transcends the large gap of time.

Anand's preoccupation with and emotional sympathy for the low and downtrodden is seen all through his fiction, particularly in *Untouchable*, *Coolie* and *The Road*, which seems to have derived from his early association with an untouchable like Bakha, strong in body and tender at heart. An episode in *Seven Summers* illustrates this. Feeling that he has been betrayed during his adventure with him, Ali slaps Krishan's face and drags him towards his follower's lanes. The young Krishan cries out and attracts Bakha, the sweeper boy, who runs to his rescue. Bakha gives a kick and cows down Ali; but he is too conscious of his low caste to pick up Krishan, and so he brings Clayton, a Christian flute player and sees to it that the boy is delivered home safe. Another time, when Krishan, an eager spectator of a '*kabaddi*' match, is hit by Ram Charan's stone, and starts howling at the sight of blood pouring down from his head, Bakha forgets or ignores all caste scruples, lifts him up and takes him to his mother's house. At home Krishan finds, to his surprise that his mother rebukes Bakha for touching and polluting him, whereas the truth is that the sweeper boy has only been a great deal more tender than others, to her son. It is instances like these that perhaps confirmed Anand's belief in the goodness of men like Bakha, despite their low-caste. It may be safely presumed that Anand has chosen only these two incidents for narration in *Seven Summers* though he must have been familiar with innumerable similar incidents. It is the artist in Anand, who saw the aptness of these two incidents as illustrating the enormous injustice underlying the caste system in India.

There is hardly any of Anand's novels which does not denounce poverty as a serious malaise which has struck the common man in India. *Coolie* may be cited as an apt illustration. Munoo becomes a tragic victim of exploitation. Poverty is the root cause of his tragedy. Similarly in *Two Leaves and a Bud* Gangu and his family join the tea-plantation of Assam, driven by poverty and hunger. Anand knows the contours of poverty from his very childhood, as is clear from *Seven Summers*. Krishan's parents, of course, do not belong to the poor class, though his father's frugality comes in the boy's way of enjoying the good things of life freely. He is thoroughly acquainted with the poverty and squalor of the inhabitants of the followers' lanes, Ram Charan, Ali, Chota and most of his other friends are poor. At Daska, his mother's village, he sees Fazlu, another poor man. These scenes of poverty and misery readily touch the chords of sympathy in the tender boy's soul and gradually make him a sure friend of the destitute and the distressed. It is his inside knowledge of the poverty and squalor in which the masses lived that makes him so human and such a rebel at heart. His initial stance as a novelist was that of the champion of the underdog. *Seven Summers* establishes that his realism is derived from his real life experiences, which he interprets imaginatively.

There is an umbilical connection between Anand's real-life experiences and his projection of them in his novels and short stories. *Seven Summers* establishes the fact that the novelist's life contained the sources of certain themes, motifs and characters of his fiction as also his fictional stance. It is no wonder then that the publisher's blurb to *Morning Face* describes *Seven Summers* as "the first part of a seven-volume long novel, *Seven Ages of Man*, a source book of the novels and stories of Mulk Raj Anand". Seven Ages of Man has relevance to Anand's fiction in that it shows how Anand's life served as the breeding ground of his "protest" philosophy. All great literature in a certain sense is protest literature and the comprehensive awareness of the sources of evil gives a writer both intensity and depth. Anand concretizes his perception of the human predicament in his age. The novelist's protest against untouchability in *Untouchable*, tragic denial of life to the poor in *Coolie*, heartless exploitation of the downtrodden in *Two Leaves and a Bud*, religious hypocrisy and tradition in the Lalu Trilogy and the plight of Indian women in *The Old Woman and the Cow* is rooted in his real life and negates the oft-repeated statement that Anand could emerge as a novelist of protest and humanism under the influence of the English Socialist movement of the thirties. It is his commitment to life that is larger than his ideological commitment that makes him a novelist of protest in India. Though the origin of Anand's sense of protest is to be seen in *Seven Summers*, in a way it has been rooted in the twentieth century Indian novel. Tagore projects the predicament of the Hindu widow in *Binodini,* the problems of caste exclusiveness and orthodoxy in *Gora,* the background of the terrorist movement in *Four Chapters* and the Swadeshi struggle in *The Home and the World*. Even R.K. Narayan plays with the various hypocritical attitudes of different persons in *Malgudi* and Ramaswami's metaphysical quest for liberation underscores the essential difference in the fundamental culture of East and West. Anand, in this perspective, stands out as an anti-*status quo* writer and Krishan Chander, his alter ego, embodies the spirit of revolt that the experience of life has bred in Anand. Krishan Chander is fully aware of his mother's early marriage and rural poverty in *Seven Summers*. His elder brother's marriage by arrangement to Draupadi is something he resents bitterly. Harish's love for Mumtaz in *Morning Face* is a clear indication of his protest against arranged marriage. In *Confession of a Lover* both Krishan and his beloved Yasmin vehemently rebel against the pernicious evil of arranged marriage. His love for her is transformed into a national love. In his novels, Anand protests against corrupt social institutions, caste restriction in Hindu society, child marriage, deplorable position of women in society and many other aspects of Indian society. These issues are traced in *Seven Ages of Man* and brought into a broader relief.

REFERENCES

Anand, Mulk Raj. *Lament on Death of A Master of Arts*. Lucknow: Naya Sansar, 1939.

——. *Lines Written to an Indian Air—Essays*. Bombay: Nalanda Publication, 1949.

——. *Preface to Two Leaves and a Bud*. Bombay: Kutub-Popular, 1951.

——. *Seven Summers*. Bombay: Kutub-Popular, 1960. (All quotes of *Seven Summers* are from this edition.)

——. *Morning Face*. Bombay: Kutub-Popular, 1968.

Cowasjee, Saros. *Author To Critic: The Letters of Mulk Raj Anand to Saros Cowasjee*. Calcutta: Writers Workshop, 1973.

——. *So Many Freedoms*. Delhi: Oxford University Press, 1977.

Fox, Ralph. *The Novel and The People*. Moscow: Foreign Language Publishing House, 1956.

Gupta, G.S. Balarama. *Mulk Raj Anand: A Study of His Fiction in Humanist Perspective*. Bareilly: Prakash Book Depot, 1974.

Harrex, S.C. *The Fire and the Offering*. Calcutta: Writers Workshop, 1977.

Mehta, P.P. *Indo-Anglian Fiction: An Assessment*. Bareilly: Prakash Book Depot, 1979.

Post-colonial Discourse in Conrad's *Heart of Darkness* and Anand's *Two Leaves and a Bud*

12

G.L. Goutam

Mulk Raj Anand remained intellectually active until the very last moment of his life, though he would have turned hundred on 12th December 2004. In the write-up he had contributed a few days before his passing away that was published on the day of his demise in *The Times of India*; he deplored how the modern science had turned man into a specialized robot without having concern for arts. On the other hand, he fondly recalled the Renaissance man who had a rounded love of science and creative arts.

The above example is a fair index of the fact how intellectually awake Anand was and what concerns remained dear to his heart until he breathed his last. If we look back at the phase of his youth, we note that he was a personality with world concerns at his heart. In the heyday of Anand's youth during the thirties and forties of the twentieth century, the clash of ideologies was at its height in Europe where he stayed until 1945. Anand had made up his mind to settle down in India after having participated in the antifascist campaign in Spain as a member of the International brigade of writers and intellectuals. But it turned out to be a futile bid to save the Spanish Republic from falling into the hands of the resurgent national militarist regime. The civil war (Grugel and Rees, 1997:04) having begun in July 1936 continued up to 1939. Garcia Lorca, the popular Spanish poet and friend of Pablo Neruda had been killed by the Fascists as soon as war began in July 1936. Ralf Fox and Christopher Coudwell died fighting for the restoration of democracy in Spain. Stephen Spender, George Orwell and Anand campaigned against the Fascists in Spain.

After Spanish civil war Anand's attention was wholly occupied by the World War II. So, he put off his final return to India till the Great War was over. It's these experiences of the world war that Anand recreated in his famous anti war novel *Across the Black Waters*. He was no less shocked by the failure of coal miners' strike that was followed by general strike in England in 1926. This strike, to Anand's great dismay, was suppressed by the powerful might of the state. By the mid-thirties, he had lived in London and Europe for nearly a decade as he reached London in 1925 to pursue his studies in philosophy. He was awarded a doctorate in philosophy on realism of Hume and his predecessors. Moreover, Marxism as a philosophical argument, he felt, could resolve the entangled philosophical questions which he had begun to grapple with when he was a student of philosophy at Khalsa College, Amritsar during 1920s. Anand was intoxicated by the heady wine of international socialism before he published his first novel *Untouchable* in 1935, which was followed by *Coolie* in 1936 and *Two Leaves and a Bud* in 1937. Hot and impetus, as Shelley felt under the power of the West wind, so did Anand feel under the impact of the revolutionary awareness of change that these works erupted out from his creative being like lava from a volcano. Significantly, Anand in *Coolie* and *Two Leaves and a Bud* attacked respectively the callous class system and colonialism, especially in *Two Leaves and a Bud*, he attacked, to use Edward W. Said phrase, 'colonial culture'. By publishing his early novels in England obviously for Western public, he aimed to show them how headless violence, ruthless suppression and naked exploitation was carried out in the British Indian colony, like its counterparts across the world under the veneer of so-called advanced culture which the English colonial system professed to represent. In 1930s, Anand had an international mission ahead of him to free from the colonial domination all the suppressed masses and nations, wherever they were. So, what Anand's noted critic Saros Cowasjee says, "International Socialism seemed to him, as it did to every progressive writer of the time, the only solution to the world problems" (1977:12). Another famous critic of Anand, Margaret Berry also remarks how Anand had association with world personalities imbued with novel vision and consciousness: "Reinforcing Anand's intellectual commitment to Western and modernist thought in these early days of his career were friendship and association with thinkers such as Eric Gill, Bonamy Dobree, E.M. Forster, D.H. Lawrence, Henry Miller, Herbert Read, Andre Malraux and Pablo Neruda" (XV, 06). He had seen the world intellectuals such as Maxim Gorky, Romain Rolland, Thomas Mann and E.M. Forster assemble in Paris in 1935. They came together to raise the voice of liberty and equality. Anand was a charter member of the all India Progressive Writers Association founded in London in 1935. According to Margaret Berry (Berry, XV, 06) its objectives were as follows:

1. It is the duty of Indian writers to give expression to the changes in Indian life and to assist the spirit of progress in this country by introducing scientific rationalism in literature. They should undertake to develop an attitude of literary criticism which will discourage the general reactionary and revivalist tendencies on question like family, religion, sex, war and society, and to combat literary trends reflecting communalism and exploitation of man by man.
2. It is the object of our association to rescue literature from the conservative classes to bring the arts into closest touch with the people.
3. We believe that the new literature of India must deal with the basic problems of poverty, social backwardness and political subjection.
4. All that arouses in us the critical spirit, which examines customs and institutions in the light of reason which helps us to organize ourselves to transform, we accept as progressive.

As a progressive writer, Anand had seen the vision of freeing India from the colonial political domination. On a perusal of *Two Leaves and a Bud* emerges a full-fledged view of post-colonial argument. Just as for Jean Paul Sartre, colonialism was a system so it is for Anand. In *Two Leaves and a Bud* the

British tea planters representing the colonial interests are masters of the land having monopolized the raising of tea, which is a natural product of Assam valley. The other resources, the labour force, who have been evicted from the land are being forced to bear the exploitation carried out by their better ones. They are violently suppressed so that they can never raise their heads by way of human dignity as they are in great number. With justice on their side, the white men as masters of land, business, with strong back up of military power and air force, are committing all conceivable crimes on Indian Coolies, who belong to the category of native "others". Moreover, colonialism as a system is characterized by the feeling of West being the only intellectually superior, physically strong and the dispenser of justice and the giver of civilization to the colonized. The colonized "other" deserves to be kept in check by force as they are culturally barbarians. The colonizers in *Two Leaves and a Bud* profess how this business of tea cultivation is gainful to the natives.

Not only is *Two Leaves and a Bud* a powerful exposition of the colonizer's culture deriving its strength from the cult of gun, but the novel ends putting a question mark on the judicial system set up under the colonial system. As an imaginative construct, the novel recreates how the colonial power is committing brutalities on the native Indians. Edward W. Said forcefully argues how the Westerns who considered themselves as givers of order in colonies committed brutal acts of violence.

> Dismissed or forgotten were the ravaged colonial people who for centuries endured summary justice, unending economic oppression, distortion of their social and intimate lives and a resource less submission that was the function of unchanging European superiority. Only to keep in mind the millions of Africans who were supplied to slave trade is to acknowledge the unimaginable cost of maintaining superiority. (Said, 1994:22)

Edward W. Said has also appreciated the fact that the scholars from former British colonies have come up with post-colonial argument. Said remarks:

> For the first time Westerners have been required to confront themselves not simply as the Raj but as representatives of a culture and even of races accused of crimes, crimes of violence, crimes of suppression, crimes of consciences. (195)

Thus, seen against the theoretical constructs enunciated by Jean Paul Sartre, Fanon and Edward W. Said *Two Leaves and a Bud* is an anti-colonial work. If Edward had taken notice of Anand's *Two Leaves and a Bud* as he had done Joseph Conrad's novella *Heart of Darkness*, he would have included it along with *Heart of Darkness* in *Culture and Imperialism* among the anti-colonial texts without reservations. In critiquing *Heart of Darkness*, Said had appreciated Conrad for showing "the discrepancy between the official idea of empire and the remarkably disorienting actuality of Africa, Marlow unsettles the reader sense not only of the very idea of empire, but of something more basic, reality itself" (29).

Despite this appreciation of *Heart of Darkness*, Said has no reservations and forthrightly points to the limited vision of Conrad. "Conrad's tragic limitation is that even though he could see clearly that on one level imperialism was essentially pure dominance and land grabbing. He could not then conclude that imperialism had to end so that "natives could have lives free from European domination" (30).

In the above observation it can be discerned Said's expectations form a work dealing with some topical question concerning a segment of humanity. Like Said, Raymond Williams has appreciated the social content in *Heart of Darkness* and rejected the abstract interpretation of Conrad's fine novella. Raymond Williams calls the life ashore river "the reality of colonial exploitation" (144). He perceptively criticizes the "white" civilized liberal humanist ideals, (146) that recommend, "Exterminate all the brutes". Besides these aspects shown by these critics, there are some other aspects like the deeply felt humanity of Conrad for black niggers and cannibals, which has been expressed through sympathetic attitude towards them in the reactions of Marlow in *Heart of Darkness*.

Through the humanist vision of Marlow, characterized with the essential humanity towards the natives in South Africa, with interest in their natural demeanour and consideration for their gait and mien, Conrad aims to deconstruct the colonial myth about the natives as sub-human, bereft of intelligence and intelligent perception. Ironically, the white colonial masters who have launched on the mission of civilizing them as custodians of advanced European civilization are turning them into sub-human beings by behaving as they would do with beasts, keeping them hungry, naked and overworking in the name of development. We can mark this contrast between the places where they are living as sons of soil and the place where colonial programme is afoot. The further Marlow journeys into the wilderness of Africa across the river, the deeper becomes physical darkness and above all grimmer becomes moral concern aggravated by colonial shameless exploitation. The Central Station where Mr. Kurtz, the business tycoon of ivory trade, is in charge of trading post occupies center-stage. Mr. Kurtz has acquired the status of an ivory legend, the symbol of imperial exploitation at whose business center ivory comes from the villages situated into interior around the central station. Other agents of ivory stationed at stations before Kurtz's Central station in Congo feel jealous of Kurtz's extra-ordinary success as an ivory agent. This may be accounted for competition under business capitalism. But all other agents of company regard him as a genius in ivory trade. Ivory permeates everywhere along the coast of the river. Marlow himself taken away by the extra-ordinary reputation of this man tells, "Hadn't I been told if I been told in all the tones of jealousy and admiration that he had collected, bartered, swindled, or stolen more ivory than all other agents together" (134).

During his voyage on steam boat as soon as Marlow lands at the first station he is enamored of the stories about Kurtz as a miracle in ivory trade. At every station he stops over during his journey to Congo, his interest is more accentuated than at the earlier one. Marlow cannot rest from journey till he has met this legend of ivory. This legend of ivory has exploited the whole country by going on exploratory expeditions for ivory.

"You would think there was not a single tusk left either above or below the ground in the whole country" (137). In a report prepared by Kurtz for the guidance of colonizers about the natives, he has recommended that the natives, whom he calls brutes, should be exterminated.

In stark contrast to Kurtz's colonial attitude to the natives Marlow thinks of them as human beings happily rowing their boat. We feel sympathy for the natives after reading the following observation of Marlow:

> You could see from afar the white of their eyeballs glistening. They shouted, sang, their bodies streamed with perspiration, they had faces like grotesque masks these chaps; but they had bone, muscle, a wild vitality, an intense energy of movement that was as natural and true as the surf along this coast. They wanted no excuse for being there. (35)

The above reality, evoking view of the native Africans as robust men, helps in forming a construct altogether different from the colonialist project wherein they have been shown as 'Brutes'. Just opposite to the colonial distortion of them they are full of "a wild vitality", "an intense energy of movement" as have other enthusiastic human being. But later on in the text of the novel we find what colonial exploitation has turned them into. They are not beings treated even like animals. If they are animals, certainly they are not normal animals, but punished or impounded ones. Marlow notes that the construction of the railway is going on. Blast is not at all required for building railway, yet dynamites are being burst. May be, it is being done for seating fear in the hearts of the natives, who have been turned into black shadows of disease and starvation.

Conrad brings home his righteous indignation by showing the true face of reality of the black people under colonialism. Marlow as a narrator tells us:

> A slight clinking behind me made me turn my head. Sick black men advanced in a file, toiling up the path. They walked erect and slow, balancing small baskets full of earth on their heads, and the clink kept time with

> their footsteps. Black rags were wound round their loins and the short ends behind waggled to and fro like tails. I could see every rib, the joints of their limbs were like knots in a connected, each had an iron collar on his neck and all were conceding together with a chain whose bights swung between them rhythmically clinking. (40-41)

We are aware of the fact that the above diatribe against colonialism has been made by Marlow who is none other than Conrad himself voicing his hatred of imperialism under which he had served like George Orwell and therefore had first-hand experiences of the conditions of the natives in colonies. The colonized in *Heart of Darkness* is not an individual character representing a community, but the black community; more particularly the have-nots have been presented through the glimpses into their lives and conditions of living. The narrative technique does not allow Conrad to develop individual characters among the natives because Marlow as a seaman is narrating his experiences to a group of English people who naturally would be interested in the stories about the legendary heroes of Empire like Kurtz; who is ivory and profit personified.

The narrative technique Mulk Raj Anand has employed in *Two Leaves and a Bud* is of social realism with a probe into the psychology of his characters not as individuals but as representatives of the community which they belong to. Nevertheless, the spokesman of the colonized underprivileged workers of Tea gardens stretching miles in Brahmaputra valley happens to be an anti-imperialist English man having resigned from Imperial Medical Service. Now he is a doctor with tea planters. Ideologically, he represents Bolshevik viewpoint. In the 1930s Marxism was the most domineering among all political ideologies. In that period intellectuals were not averse to aligning themselves with ideologies. In this connection it is enormously important to remember that the writings Karl Marx helped a great deal of scholars to understand the colonial exploitation of India. Karl Marx in his Letters on India contributed in 1853 to *New York Herald Tribune* had prophesized that the railway the colonial powers had been building into the interiors of India had been constructed with the single objective of getting an access of cheap raw-material available there.

Christopher Caudwell and Ralf Fox were active fire-brand revolutionaries in international leftist movement and they valued peoples' democracy more than other thing. Anand projects the anti-colonial vision, through the character of De La Havre whose relations with management of tea plantation are getting strained, as the Marxist humanist doctor takes the side of the coolies who have survived on subsistence level of existence. Charles Croft-Cooke, the manager of MacPherson Tea Estate and the Assistant Manager, Reggie Hunt are the faithful servants of Tea Company with head office in England. The doctor is more popular with coolies than with the English characters, including the wife of the Manager, who in her characteristic mien keeps complaining of the heat in India.

Mrs. Croft-Cooke holds the natives in contempt. Out of her colonial contempt of them, she calls them liars who also steal. Her husband Charles Croft-Cooke is a typical English businessman. The pride of his "Englishness" has got deep seated in him through his long stay of twenty years in India. He is different from assistant planter Reggie Hunt in that he professes to value efficiency at home and work and the latter believes in the cult of committing violence on unarmed coolies. In contrast to Reggie Hunt who puts on false bravado in suppressing the demonstration of the coolies, he is a coward at heart. He is scared of the nationalist movement being spearheaded by the Congress Wallahs and no less of the terrorist outrage in Calcutta. Therefore, he carries a revolver in his pocket like other English men in India to boost up his sagging morale. Subscribing to a colonial outlook, he exercises no reticence in calling the planter coolies as sub-human; ignorant of the benefits of hygiene. Hence, the plan doctor has worked on for supply of pure water to the coolies is summarily rejected by the Manager. The humanist doctor's credence how a cup of tea contains the hunger, the sweat and despair of a million of Indians convinces one of his deep sympathy for the struggling workers. As an intellectual, he abhors tea parties. Yet ironically enough, he has to voice his intellectual credentials and take sides during these tea parties. The other contradiction in his character being that he loves an English girl, the daughter of senior planter Mr Cooke, but hates the British goods. Anand expresses his view point in the following words:

> The doctor had resisted Anglo-India's belief in British greatness ever since his arrival in this country. At first, perhaps, it had been from an instinct to be different from everyone else, an individual. Then he had given up the Imperial Medical Service, because the sentimental romanticism wanted to make a brave gesture to convince himself that he had really come to regard Indians as human beings and to believe that they have right not only to rule themselves, but to rule themselves justly by destroying the inequalities of caste, class and creed. (30)

Miss Barbara, the daughter of Manager, is the lone appreciator of De La Havre's pro-native credence as they are lovers.

In the outburst of the doctor with Barbara, Anand expresses the contempt he felt of colonialism by showing the paradoxical situation the European imperialist power created. He shows how the "Britons" who have launched upon the nefarious mission of enslaving the millions in Asia have been christened as civil and those enslaved as barbarians. He attributes the growth of industrial civilization to the "open loot and bribery and corruption" and to "dividends from the company's share." The empire of industry in Bradford and Manchester could not have been possible, but for the large fortunes from the colonies spanned across world. They exploited the natural resources coal and iron and working classes. The humanist doctor believes that nothing would have come out from the machinery invented in England, if the capital had not been looted from the colonies. The doctor's observations come akin to what post-colonial thinker Fanon believed in 1950s that Europe "built up with sweat and the dead bodies of Negroes, Arabs, Indians, and the yellow races...and Europe is literally the creation of the third world" (Fanon in Said, 1984:195).

The Manager's bungalow, standing atop a hill at the edge of widely spread tea gardens, constitutes a world apart. The coolies' settlement at edge of the stream in the basin of the valley, down the hill, represents another world where cholera visits almost every year. So the setting of *Two Leaves and a Bud* points to the existence of two worlds: one of the colonizers and other of the colonized. The English colonizers have a culture and of course, concerns altogether different from those of native coolies. The latter suffer from disease, death, and alienation as they have been brought to the tea estate from far off on the pretext of giving them land, advances of money to pay off their debts, and a brick-built house. The villages where they had lived before were not idyllic affording a cosy living either, yet the world colonizers have given them turns out to be worse than the previous existence. The colonizers drink whisky, pass their leisure in sports, go to the English clubs and enjoy horse riding. On the other hand, an indentured labourer Gangu's family of four, wife Sajni, daughter Leila and son Buddhu hardly gets two meals a day. The wages do not work out eight annas a day for the whole family. "Three annas for him, two annas for his wife and daughter and three pice for his child. Why in his village he had been able to earn eight annas a day alone by working on the landlord's land when he had lost his own" (64). Such details in the novel are reminiscent of Charles Dickens' later matured works like *Bleak House* where Dickens shows the poor living under such bad conditions as the have-nots in colonies. Like Dickens, Anand understands the have-nots' world intimately and portrays it with an in-depth understanding, a unique forte, setting him apart from his other contemporaries. All major and minor characters are rooted in reality. Gangu, since he is a labourer past his youth, cannot convince himself to settle to the new life at the colonial tea plantations, though thousands other coolies are suffering under colonial exploitation. If his essential needs had been attended to here, he would have welcomed the change. Though senior coolies share his sufferings, the beating, insults and losses he suffers have embittered him. He not only loses his wife, who stood to him through thick and thin of life, following the outbreak of cholera, but also suffers insults at the hands of the colonizers, for he cannot afford the last rites expenses of his wife. Sajni's death leaves Gangu disdraught; somehow, he comes to terms with callous fate, pinning his hope on his lovely daughter whose character has been drawn with full awareness of her sensitive nature as a responsible girl. During a visit to market place at the tea plantation she puts off buying a nose ring and bangle as the family is short of money. Anand calls her "an elfin spirit wedded to the air" (68). As a sensitive girl, she should not add to the burden of expenses on her father who she feels, has been swindled by the contractor of the plantation. Though Gangu has believed the concocted talks of Buta Ram and finds himself in barless prison at the tea plantation, the suffering has made him wiser and at the first glance can he see how the culture of bribery prevails everywhere under the colonial rule.

> ...He was convinced that Buta had promised the babu a bribe. And he began to fear that, as in district court of Hoshiarpur, so here an atmosphere of twisting and turning prevailed. (13-14)

Just as colonial management believes how some of the coolies return as landlords, so the colonial project of construction is afoot in *Heart of Darkness* which is considered to be a gift from the colonial masters. The workers living under this project have been brought from afar all parts of South Africa. To quote Conrad's own words:

> Brought from all the recesses of the coast in all the legality of time contracts, lost in uncongenial surroundings fed on unfamiliar food, they sickened, became inefficient, and then allowed to crawl away and rest. (45)

Against the shocking conditions social existence of natives in colonial South Africa, the White Accountant of the Irony Company has been shown dressed in snowy white outfit, a self-engrossed man, cruel from skin to the bone. When busy with book-keeping, no iota of sympathy ever visits him, even if the natives continue to die in his very presence. In *Two Leaves and a Bud*, we have the White Accountant's counterpart in Reggie who may justly be called the devil of violence, a terror-incarnate. Whereas Manager Croft-Cooke has earned a respectability among the natives by keeping himself aloof from them, Reggie Hunt has achieved the identical objective by creating a terror of being an English Sahib among the dispossessed coolies. Since they are essentially businessmen engaged in agricultural industry, they look upon each other with suspicion as there is business jealousy between the Manager and Kurtz in *Heart of Darkness*. In order to keep his prestige up among them, Reggie has no qualms about flogging them on slight provocation or a lapse in picking up leaves from a tea plant. Just as the bourgeois culture characteristically breeds violence, so did the colonial culture everywhere derives its strength from the culture of creating terror. Anand has devoted a considerable part of the text to show how all the servants of the company, backed up by the military and airforce, put down with iron hand what they call the mutiny of the coolies, though it all begins as an altercation between two labourer women. The squabble takes such a turn that army and airforce have to be called in to slow down the plantation coolies. Reggie has to be blamed for matter assuming such alarming proportion, since he believes the natives to be quarrelsome and uncivilized and mishandles the situation from the very beginning. The babbling, shouting, gesticulating coolies who have gathered on the spot of quarrel from all over the valley following the quarrel are ordered to be caned and Reggie rides his horse over them causing them serious hurt. After this follows the riot of the coolies who are inhumanly lathi-charged, bedraggled and belaboured, resulting in death of some coolies. The spirited among the coolies take a demonstration to the Sahab's bungalow as they have been boosted to do so by Doctor De La Havre whom the coolies regard as their *mai-baap*. After this headless violence on the unarmed coolies, the doctor recalls that the poor coolies are as inhumanly suppressed in "*vilayat*" as here in colonies. They are forced back on the threats of being shot dead and the warders drive the men back with the barrel-ends of their rifles.

The violence already done to the coolies is not enough punishment for their wrongs. They as a barbarian tribe need to be taught a lesson so that they may not think of rioting or demonstrating in the future. As planned by the English planters and the army, the aeroplanes ordered from the British Indian Air Force fly over the coolies' settlement in order to seat in their hearts the fear of Almighty imperial power in India. Coolies feel panicked as one coolie pregnant woman dies out of fear.

At a time the intellectuals in India believed that the British judicial dispensation in India was based on the principle of equality treating on equal footing the persons of all castes and communities in India. But Anand seems to demolish this notion of English law being fair to all in India and shows the colonial character of administration of justice. The novel ends at shocking note how Reggie is held guiltless of the murder of Gangu who thwarted the attempt of Reggie to rape his daughter Leila.

To conclude Anand and Joseph Conrad's concerns with regard to colonialism; Conrad and Anand were filled with an overwhelming sense of outrage. Anand's concern for the dispossessed went across the national boundaries and included the dispossessed of England, an imperialist power herself. The English culture and civilization, as has been shown by Fanon, did not bring within its civilizing fold the underprivileged masses in England. Writers like Dickens were concerned about them and showed that they, too, belonged to the category of the colonized. As regards Conrad's vision of colonialism, Said has found it in adequate, as he wanted Conrad to allow in the texture of *Heart of Darkness* political freedom to the natives of Africa. But if we take into account the Marxian critical standards, the whole Marxist aesthetics no where approves of preaching a political philosophy, as the political thinkers do. Marx was even against preaching a revolution. He wanted the creative writer to show the contradictions of the system, the difference between what the writer wants to prevail and what actual life conditions obtain. Conrad deeply engages the reader in the reality of exploitations by removing the mask under which the truth lay hidden and the reader comes to have a shared perception of hatred of colonialism Conrad so deeply experienced.

Since post-colonialism is an oppositional argument based upon such binary oppositions as dominations/subordination, the colonizer/the colonized, the empire/the nation, the central/ peripheral, it has come under attack from the Western scholars. Robert Young, an Oxford academic, questions the politics of post-colonial discourse in these words, "The rise of post-colonial study coincided with the end of Marxism as the defining political, cultural and economic objective in much of the third world. But if it still seeks an oppositional role, what form of critical participatory economics should post-colonial analysis look to?" (Young in Rao, 2003:09).

In the above argument the pronouncement of the end of Marxism and linking it with the rise of post-colonial argument as an alternative has been made in the fashion of much of the post-modern argument. But the fact remains that the study of Marx has not only enabled the post-colonial theoreticians like Fanon, Sartre, Edward Said to underscore the colonial exploitation, but Marx stands more relevant now than before for countering the global capitalism. The socialist movements are again resurgent in third world, and globalisation is under fire everywhere. Professor Rao answers the above charges more cogently: "Here it could be even pointed out that 'Marx' at least in certain parts of India in this period, did not come simply from above as such.... The persistence of Marxian notes can be distinctly identified in the social movements—largely composed of the marginalized and grass-roots communities. The haunting of Marx from below is still palpable in the Indian context" (10). So post-colonial discourse seeks not only to correct the distortion of history committed by the colonized European out of imperialist ambitions, but as an oppositional argument it joins the political movements like Marxism to clamber for justice to the subaltern categories.

REFERENCES

Anand, Mulk Raj. *Two Leaves and a Bud* (1937). New Delhi: Arnold Publishers, 1983.

Berry, Margaret. 'Two Faces of Indo-Anglian Fiction: Mulk Raj Anand and R.K. Narayan', *South Asian Review*, Vol. XV, Florida.

Cowasjee, Saros. *So Many Freedoms*. Bombay: Oxford University Press, 1977.

Conrad, Joseph. *Heart of Darkness*. Gurgaon: PBD publications (edition's year not given).

Fanon Quoted in Edward W. Said. *Culture and Imperialism*. New York: Vintage Books, 1994.

Grugel, Jean and Tim Rees. *Franco's Spain*. London: Arnold, 1997. They write about the civil war in Spain: "From the outbreak of the war in July 1936, dictatorial rule became established in all those areas which came under the control of Nationalist forces. The political structures, which were to be established throughout the country after 1939, were erected during the conflict itself. For its entire later day politics, and frequently the policies of the regime were conditioned by this struggle to control the destiny of Spain and the relationship between the state and its citizens for nearly 40 years was largely created between 1936 and 1939.

Rao, D. Venket. "Political Returns: Abuses of the Academy" in Sukalpa Bhattacharjee (ed.) *Post-Colonial Theory and Literature*. New Delhi: Atlantic Publishers and Distributors, 2003.

Said, Edward W. *Culture and Imperialism*. New York: Vintage Books, 1994.

Williams, Raymond. *The English Novel: From Dickens to Lawrence*. London: The Hogarth Press, 1984.

Young, Robert. Quoted in D. Venket Rao "Political Returns: Abuses of the Academy" in Sukalpa Bhattacharjee ed. *Post-Colonial Theory and Literature*. New Delhi: Atlantic Publishers and Distributors, 2003.

The Subaltern Strain in *Untouchable*

13

Syed Afroz Ashrafi

Towards the end of the 20th century a phrase was coined commonly referred to as *Dalit* literature and with each passing day the phrase assumed complexity of dimensions and directions with a host of writers emerging on the literary scene to be the prophets of the so-called *Dalit* literature. Across the globe the wind blew and the society of different hues examined. In the wider perspective, initially it was seen in terms of racial prejudice harboured by the superior breed of people and self-acclaimed bourgeoisie phantoms who guided the destiny of the human society; and imposed codes of conduct to be followed by every single citizen but not without raising walls and boundaries of segregation; ostracism and insulation. Amidst such proclaimed and visible bias there came about a cluster of writers such as Chinua Achebe, Coetzee, Osman Berrada, Mungoshi, Edward Said and Alia Riffat from the African continent; who were engaged relentlessly in the evaluation of those reeling under the wails and cries manufactured by the privileged creatures. Alex La Guma raised the banner of protest and in the process laid down the foundation stone of protest literature. This spectacle could not remain confined to Africa alone and gradually it filtered down to the East that provided even a more productive and fertile land to let flourish the literature of the same brand with identical issues and concerns. Urdu and Hindi fiction in particular showed enough urgency of reason and purpose to write about those crushed under the imposing boots of racial prejudice; as writers like Ghazanfar, Syed Mohammed Ashraf and Wajahat Sagheer picked up this thread to weave around their fictional structure, to make stories and expose the double faced human society. In Hindi fiction also, there are voices steeped in sobs and surrender, the will to trudge the unconventional paths and the might to tame the tradition of barbarian society; that has built a hype and gloss around its existence. Jabir Hussain also shares the dais with the select group of writers, known in general literary parlance as the commentator of the *Dalits*.

My concern here is to dismantle the thesis that the advocates of the suppressed were born in the African continent whether it is apartheid or struggle for freedom for such concerns were even more prominent in Indo-Anglican writings; and the writer to take to such writings and expose the gory faced, stony hearted monster of the society, having created too many taboos, guided by an ideology too cruel to survive in a society is Mulk Raj Anand. In fact the so-called *Dalit* literature has its root in Indo-Anglican fiction and the genesis of such writings could well be traced back to 1935 when Anand wrote his first novel *Untouchable*, followed by *Coolie* in 1936. Together these two novels if seen in totality fully qualify and deserve to be clubbed with subaltern group.

Mulk Raj Anand is no ordinary name in the realm of Indo-Anglican fiction as his contribution is as profound and monumental as that of R.K. Narayan and Raja Rao and the very few could have anticipated then that the first stone R.K. Narayan cast in Indo-Anglican fiction would lead to an array of writers converging on the fictional scene and will be stretched to the extent that will culminate into *The Hungry Tide* of Amitav Ghosh and *Shalimar The Clown* of Salman Rushdie. Here my objective is to attempt a modest evaluation of Mulk Raj Anand's *Untouchable* and to try and find the subaltern dimensions. My aim is confined to the analysis of the novel in question and to discover how Anand's mind went down to the root of a serious menace which in retrospect today has become a fashionable coffee house discussion. Anand has a body of creative corpus to his credit that went a long way in determining the direction of the Indo-Anglican fiction. Together with R.K. Narayan he created and introduced Indian English fiction to the world outside not as mere imitator of the western masters but had a genuine talent for creativity that did eventually earn him the epithet of the man with a rolling and wagging tongue and rode a crest of unparallel publicity in Indian literary history and beyond.

E.M. Forster writes in the Preface to *Untouchable*:

> *Untouchable* could only have been written by an Indian, and by an Indian who observed from the outside no European however sympathetic, could have created the character of Bakha, because he would not have known enough about his troubles. (vii)

This observation is made by the writer of *A Passage to India* who did his best to dismantle the chasm between the East and West. But ironically, he failed in his honest attempt to discover the real India only to be dismissed as muddle by the western imagination at large. The very line that *Untouchable* could only have been written by an Indian and is a recognition of the fact that Anand knew exactly what he wanted to write and how hard and difficult it might have been to see the disdainfully outcaste treated so realistically through the razor sharp imagination of Anand. *Untouchable* indeed is the by-product of human conduct induced through the caste system authored though by a cunning and chiselled sculptor of society. The novel is a moving pathetic tale of an individual pushed to the brink of a society that uses, abuses and discards him for having belonged to that strata of the Hindu society, which has a time-tested belief in exploitation and sustained through an inborn prejudice against a fellow citizen. Anand's narrative, craftsmanship and his amazing proximity to an abused individual, known as Bakha in the novel, leaves nothing to be desired.

Iyengar (1985:333) claims that "the nineteen thirties were the seed-time of modern independent India, the Gandhian salt *satyagraha* movements of 1930 and 1932, the three round table conferences, the passing of the Government of India Act of 1935, the introduction of Provincial Autonomy in 1937, the Gandian movements for *Harijan* uplift and basic education, the organisation of Marxist parties of diverse hues, the Congress Socialists, the Royalists, the Communists, the involvement in the war in 1939, the Schism in the Congress leading to the expulsion of Subhas Chandra Bose and his eventual escape to Germany and Japan—it was a packed decade indeed". Though normally resided in England, Anand too could not but respond to the impact of events in India. With him however, as with Bankim Chandra Chatterjee before him, political action took the form of writing novels. He wrote of the people, for the people and as a man of the people. It may be said that these early novels reveal an aim and a sense of direction much as an avalanche or a flood shows a fury of momentum, a surge of force, a heady rush towards the God. Evidently here a novelist, in a hurry, who must say all that he has to say as quickly, and as effectively as he can. As effectively as he can is a reference to the powerful narrative, the life like dimensions that Bakha has and the ugly face of the society's barbarian intent.

Consider what Iyengar further argues:

> Thus when Anand started writing fiction he decided he would prefer the familiar to the fancied, that he would avoid the highways of romance and sophistication but explore the by-lane of the outcastes and the peasants, the sepoys and the working people. It was, however, no laborious exercise of self-conscious proletarianism. To Anand it was merely the easier and more natural way; he was himself of the proletariat, if you will and he wrote in a brisk unself-conscious way about what he had seen at first-hand in the years of his childhood, boyhood and youth. (335)

This provides inkling about Anand's mental mould, the ability to observe and write without prejudice and the evolution of a natural concern towards those combating the excesses of a superficial society whose wings flutter to intimidate the lesser mortals ostracised for the sake of personal gratification. Bakha, the central character of the novel, is neither a tragic protagonist nor a stoical figure but a tortured individual whose soul is into shreds. Anand, therefore, in *Untouchable* naturally qualifies to be a proletarian commentator, who does not say sorry, but feels it.

The novel opens with a reference to the introduction of the outcaste colony; its physical description and the minor details to inform the reader at the very outset about the way he would explode on such a ticklish issue, the lot of the subaltern or say the plight of the emaciated and the downtrodden.

> The outcaste colony was a group of mud-walled houses that clustered together in two rows, under the shadow of both the town and cantonment, but outside their boundaries and separate, from them. There lived the scavengers, the leather workers, the ashermen, the barbers, the water carriers, the grass cutters and other outcastes from the Hindu society. (01)

This description brings to mind the photographic fidelity of how those victims of a lopsided social system live. On the skirts of town or village, their existence is a reminder of what they are, how they are discarded from the mainstream to live as abandoned creatures.

> Atleast so thought Bakha, a youngman of eighteen, strong and able-bodied, the son of Lakha, the jemadar of all the sweepers in the town and the cantonment, and officially in charge of the three rows of public latrines which lined the extreme end of the colony, by a brookside. (01)

Bakha is introduced to the reader in the very first page of the book and from there Anand never loses sight of this character so rich, vivid, pregnant with an illusory vision and false hopes.

"But Bakha was a child of modern India" (02), who tells enough about what Anand had in mind while delineating him. Bakha, though out and out an outcaste, acutely aware of his wretched origin and enduring the travails of humiliation heaped upon him day and night, but was equally determined to recast himself, pledged to a commitment to go for a transition in his own life, to build his own destiny regardless of how hard and tough the road ahead him is. Even his father's invectives did not deter him, instead instilled him into a confidence that never existed in actuality. The honest confession that he was the lowest of the low, born to serve people of high castes and to remain servile did anguish his soul. His wild fantasies, lingoes and adventures did not act as impediments to the realisation that he has a right to be a dream merchant.

> He had begged one Tommy for the gift of a pair of trousers. The man had given him a pair of breeches which he had to spare. (03)

Bakha has had every desire to be the one like Tommy, to be a gentleman, to be loved and respected the way a sepoy or Tommy is honoured. Anand in the portrayal of Bakha draws upon every minor detail to project the dreams and desires, the wishes and urges of a downtrodden, who everyday builds pictures that stands castled at the end of the day. How tough and ridiculous the existence of an outcaste is, could be gauged from the fact that his every attempt to look different from his clan borders on an imaginative flight of fancy and highways to romance comes crashing down in eventual realisation that he is born to lead a life of humiliation orchestrated by the Babus of the society that does little precious to think about effecting any catharsis with regard to a downtrodden's existence. The two events in his life have a permanent scar and abandon his dreams to dustbin. First, Sohini his sister's modesty being outraged by a priest and given the reluctance of the girl to concede what the priest did and how she defiled the priest but the priest goes scot free. The cries of "posh, posh, sweeper coming" torment his soul and bemuse him to the extent that he begins to hate his entire existence. In Bakha, Anand has exposed the blatant and macabre designs of those self-appointed conscience keepers of the Hindu society who wallow in mud and slush and create divisions on the social level that further compound the agony of the marginalised. Look at his submission.

> Bakha was shy, knowing he had no right to indulge in such luxuries as apeing the high caste people. He humbly mumbled; Huzoor it is all your blessing. Charat Singh was feeling kind, though he did not relax, the grin which symbolised six thousand years of racial and class superiority. (08)

Six thosands years of racial and class superiority can suffice to tame into timidity the meek resistance, and can induce an invincible complex into the psyche of a battered creature like Bakha. Many boots trampled over him, umpteen abuses pierced through his tender and sensitive heart and coerced into servility without any grudge. Anand goes deep into the soul of a besmirched individual who does not look beyond the life of broom and basket. Castigated for imitating styles and condemned for trying to raise head above the permissible heights. The wanton saga of Bakha is the result of the brazen *Manuvadi* mentality created to torment the existence of the low-born. How sensitive an artist Anand is, can be realised after one has carefully outlined what he meant by creating a character like Bakha who is not only a destitute, but also the butt of ridicule of all and sundry. The traumatised, scornful and merciless societal conduct towards a fellow citizen is the stigma, a real blot on the glossy but hollow face of a remorseless society.

Bakha is a representation not of bare facts associated with Dalit existence, but a sordid projection of an evil, of a stigma, and of the ferocity the bias is frought with. It is to the credit of Anand that he creates splendid images of squalor, dirt and filth with splendid indifference. The understanding of such a social squalor reflects Anand's proximity towards those discarded disdainfully by the hypocritical nature of the human conduct.

Consider Iyengar's opinion in this regard:

> There is no doubt that he has drawn upon what he had seen and heard as a boy, for there is a photographic fidelity about the picture that convinces at once, though it also overwhelms us by its cumulative ferocity and force of detail. (vii)

The photographic fidelity that Iyengar refers to is an allusion to the mass of experiences and observations, which Anand had in his kitty and to manipulate such experiences into fiction cannot be possible without the necessary fictional prowess, the imaginative coherence and the ability to tell tale with such amazing authority and incomparable clarity. The Dalit tales are much in vogue today, almost customary and fashionable to talk about dalit literature, a trend that every writer is trying to hold on but what has been discussed today, was well anticipated by Mulk Raj Anand way back in 1935 and the two novels *Untouchable* and *Coolie* speak volumes about what Anand had visualised and written in them. Bakha is one of the thousand characters, one among many and so is Monuaa of *Coolie*, who is destined to be in servitude for centuries together, whom Gandhi called the Harijans, the children of God and thus crime committed against them is the crime against humanity. The fact, however, is different. Bakha is a painful portrait of an individual in distress, representative of the social indignation whose world of fancy survives for a brief period, whose dream is crushed under the ruthless weight of social contradictions and is born to serve. The face of India may have changed, the visionaries and builders of modern India may have gone euphoric but the unpalatable fact remains that Bakha is still there in some form or the other.

Though the novel was written in 1935 but the nature and dimension of the problem perhaps was not as serious as today. Until yesterday it was a problem only. Today it is a social menace; a pariah and the problem of "untouchability" did not die with Anand or Gandhi. It is more relevant in the context of today's social structure where the chasm between the high and low is ever so widening, where the proletarian is more pronounced a proletarian and the bourgeoisie, a more pronounced bourgeoisie.

Today there are hundred thousand Bakhas who are denied access to dreams and condemned eternally to a life of abuse and humiliation. The *Manuvadis* are persisting with their satanic designs, the Brahmins stick even harder to obduracy and those marginalised are still waiting for the re-surrection of prophets to have their lots redeemed. The novel's idea is no longer radically novel nor the solutions in sight save and except to see them as a body of people who could be used for political ends. They are limping individuals delivered from the subaltern wombs. The subaltern strain in *Untouchable* is clearly evident and Anand is the author of Dalit literature that may have assumed diverse hues today. But Anand in general casts the first stone of Dalit fiction. Bakha and Monuaa are metaphors today. May be, there are people writing on such themes but to create a Bakha or Monuaa cannot be the business of an ordinary imagination.

REFERENCES

Anand, Mulk Raj. *Untouchable*. New Delhi: Penguin Books, 2001.

Foster, E.M. 'Preface' to *Untouchable*. New Delhi: Penguin Books, 2001.

Iyenger, K. Srinivas, ed. 'Mulk Raj Anand' in *Indian Writing in English*. New Delhi: Sterling Publication Pvt. Ltd., 1985.

Voice of the Voiceless: Gauri in Mulk Raj Anand's *The Old Woman and the Cow*

14

Malti Agarwal

Indian writing in English emerged as an offshoot of English Literature but soon it established itself as different from all other literatures. It became a powerful medium in the hands of the Indian writers to relate their native feelings in foreign medium. Needless to say, gradually it appeared perfectly as indigenous literature since the themes considered by these native writers were closely connected with the woes and worries, tears and smiles of the native people.

Indian writers attempted almost all major literary genres, fiction being in the forefront since the novel suits the Indian temper the most. The Indian English Literature with a history of almost a century is richly dipped in the hues of native cultural ethos. It gives voice to the prevalent malpractices in the contemporary Indian societies. The literary gamut of the Indian writers writing in English is imbued with the writers' voice against the exploitation of the downtroddens and the destitutes, the untouchables and the poverty-stricken poor lot. Women, being one important marginalized class, won the sympathy of these writers as they have always been exploited by their male partners in the name of religion or social customs. The writers like Mulk Raj Anand, R.K. Narayan, Bhabani Bhattacharya, Kamala Markandaya and others vividly depicted such female figures who, on the one hand, are patience and tolerance incarnate, undergoing all sorts of injustice and yet uncomplaining but, on the other hand, they emerge out as strong individuals, challenging all traditional taboos.

Mulk Raj Anand, one of the founding fathers of Indian English literature, a winner of many national and international prestigious awards, including the Padma Bhushan, signified the dawn of a new era in Indian English literature. He seems to raise a voice of protest against persecution of women in his writings. This voice of protest becomes more apparent in his novel *The Old Women and the Cow* (first published in 1960), which was later published in 1981 with the title *Gauri,* a heroine oriented novel. Commenting on the character of Gauri, the novelist himself writes that *Gauri* "is my offering to the beauty, dignity and devotion of Indian women".

In traditional and conventional Indian society, a woman is supposed to be docile, an apostle of love and sacrifice and silent sufferer of patriarchal rage, male chauvinism, sexual oppression, colonial mind set of males and so on. She becomes a victim not only of man's inhuman attitude but also of a system—the Hindu Dharma, which maintains that a wife is her husband's property or his possession and she has no individuality outside that system. But the spread of education and economic independence have provoked women to raise their voice against this exploitation, fight against the present social set-up and assert their rights. Anand's Gauri in *The Old Woman and the Cow*, though illiterate, defies this conventional mode of tradition-bound society and finally walks out of the sacrosanct institution of marriage. Like Ibsen's Nora, she becomes conscious of her self-esteem and breaks through age-old traditions.

Women in Indian society have been treated as the other self or man's subordinate. She is thought to be a play thing in the hands of man. The male protagonist, Panchi, in *The Old Woman and the Cow* confirms this age-old belief. Panchi is overjoyed with the prospect of marrying a girl who "is like a cow, very gentle and very good" (11) and "whom he could fold in his arms at night and kick during the day, who would adorn his house and help him with the land" (11). Gauri silently suffers and ungrudgingly "puts up with everything at her husband's home and settles down patiently to a life of unremitting toil, hunger, and pain" (Sinha, 68).

The orthodox family of Panchi considers Gauri ominous and holds her responsible for the widespread drought and famine in the village. The gentle, cow like Gauri remains deaf and dumb to all these allegations. The crisis occurs when the quarrel between uncle Mole Ram and Panchi leads to the break up of the joint family and the blame of it is put on Gauri. Panchi yells, "...ohe, only after I married have all my troubles begun..." (32) and again, "She has ruined me, Ohe Sone! Ohe Chandi! She has destroyed our home, this, Gauri..." (33). Kesaro, the aunt of Panchi, also considers Gauri the incarnation of the Goddess Kali, "the black goddess" who brings famine and disaster in the village. Gauri's meekness makes Kesaro assure that she would be able to arouse any suspicion in Panchi against her. Even her chastity is doubted. This tyrannical behaviour of her mother-in-law and the beatings at the hands of her husband rouse the spark of revolution in her and she whispers, "Patience—how long can I go on being patient against the nagging of that woman and your shoe beatings on her behalf!" (44-45). This 'gentle cow' roused to such a pitch of clear speech. A woman who was reticent and always "remained shrunk in the shell of her own demure little personality, shy and hesitant and even afraid of him" (75) (Panchi) and who believed that a woman was all for her husband to take or to reject her just as he liked, now has fits of anger. She shouts at Kesaro, "Get out of my house, Witch! Get out. You oppressed me enough when I first came as a bride. Until you and your husband turned us out. Now don't come interfering in our lives. If you have no husband, go to someone else, but do not lay hands on my husband.... Go, get out ! ...Evil woman! you want two husbands! your own for bearing you and mine for loving you. Acha, I won't give you my husband! So go..." (95). Neither Kesaro nor Panchi could ever thought Gauri capable of this. Gauri sparkles with this sudden flashing power that had come into her, turning her into Kali, the 'divine destroyer'.

The Old Woman and the Cow portrays the two diametrically opposite virtues of Gauri's personality. She, on the one hand, brings forth the image of the black Goddess who fights against injustice but, on the other hand, her image of a self-sacrificing, self-effacing woman who concedes to her subjugation with a spirit of nonchalance becomes evident. Gauri, the heroine, believed in the worship of her lord and master and wanted ultimately to conquer him with her devotion (100) like an ideal Indian wife. She remembered the songs of Mira Bai and thought that she could get to Panchi through her devotion. But Gauri was conscious of her individuality also as she adopted the modernistic view of love. One day she woke him up by making a verbal appeal—"Utho nan. Panchiji, Utho!" It was really an act of bravado which no Hindu wife dares to make.

The revelation of Gauri's pregnancy plunged Panchi into a "veritable whirlpool of doubts" and kicking her badly, he said: "Go to your mother's home, you of the evil stars!" (102). And finally despite her requests, she was sent back to her mother's home in the village of Piplan Kalan: Her misery did not come to an end rather something worse happened when his uncle Amru sold her to Seth Jai Ram Das, a rich old man of Hoshiarpur. No doubt, she resisted the advances of his uncle who caught hold of her by the plait of her hair, dragged her down from the bed. Gauri became red with rage "like that of Kali in anger" (126). She shouted as she had the flames of the Goddess Kali in her:

> "Go away and eat the ashes!...Monster! Don't torment me!..." (127)

Gauri emerges as a new woman who does not follow the age-old traditions of the society blindly. She reacts pungently to the hypocrisy of the people who cover their sexual desires under the garb of religiosity or attempt to seduce the young girls as if "sanctifying rape with holy verses" (134). Gauri did not surrender to the love advances of Seth Jai Ram Das and when once he tried to molest her she resisted angrily, sought shelter in the clinic of Colonel Mahindra. But her miseries didn't come to an end. Dr. Batra, the Colonel's partner, attempted to rape her. Once again she saved herself from this abduction by her strong resistance. Colonel Mahindra made her a nurse and restored her to her husband. But Gauri's stay at Panchi's barn now raised the brows of the villagers and invited criticism. The village gossips tormented Panchi and he asked Gauri to prove her chastity, if she could. When Panchi asked her, "What is the proof of your purity?", Gauri said, "I have been true to you." When Gauri decided to walk out of Panchi's life, hit by Panchi, she said defiantly, "Acha, if I am a curse upon you, I will go away....

I shall go and work in Daktar Mahindra's hospital and have my child there. And I will not come back again" (263). Mark the transformation which takes place in Gauri at this juncture of life. She exhibited terrible strength when she shrieked, "And if you strike me again, I will hit you back...."

Gauri is the "incarnation of Sita" (Sinha, 69) but she is not self-sacrificing like Sita. When her self-esteem is hurt, she becomes a rebel as she registers her protest against Panchi's injustice and calls him a coward who pretended to be a lion among the men of the village. She retorts angrily, "They are telling him that Ram turned out Sita because everyone doubted her chastity during her stay with Ravana!...I am not Sita that the earth will open up and swallow me. I shall just go out and be forgotten of him..." (263). To quote Jack Lindsay, "Here the key-pattern lies in the tale from *The Ramayana* of the wife who is banished because she had innocently lived in another man's house. Gauri...breaks through. The blind circle is ended. The woman who is banished becomes the woman who herself rejects the narrow world of subjections and fears that enslave Panchi despite his better self" (Lindsay, 29).

Gauri, though meek "like a cow, very gentle and very good", had the seeds of a new woman in her who has learnt not only to discharge her duties but also to assert her rights. She like an ideal Indian wife loves her husband and stands erect like a rock before all crises. The novelist vividly describes her struggle which she makes to conquer her own weakness when she resolves to leave her husband's home: "Her face shone from the pressure of her stricken heart, transfigured from the gentle cow's acquiescent visage of the time when she had arrived in Panchi's house, to that of a woman—with a will of her own, though her heart palpitated with every step" (264).

Gauri's stay at Doctor's clinic had made her wise and also aware of malpractices, prevailing in the village. Gauri, when she first came to her husband's house, had no tongue in her mouth. She simply did house work and wept on her cot. She could not think. But inner transformation of Gauri enabled her to analyse the present state of the villagers. She quotes Doctor Mahindra, "Where there is poverty there is a money—lender, a priest and a landlord—and God is always on their side" (240). To her, the gambling and the borrowing, the drinking and the wife beating are the great enemies of man. Anand imparts a message to the Indian society, i.e. how the spread of education can set the Indian society free from the clutches of superstitions, orthodox beliefs and so on. Gauri said quoting Doctor "Education will make us master fate" (241). She, like Paro, seems to believe, "There is neither Devi nor Kali! There is only one's own strength..." (115). Her decision to work as a nurse in Doctor's clinic (be economically self-reliant) equips her with moral strength and she deserts her husband which indicates that there is a change in her earlier notions. One of her earlier notions was that woman is for suffering: "Suffering for us, sister, suffering, only suffering for us women" (116). She fights back against the traditional attitude of society where people like the "sons and son's son and consider girls a curse".

Gauri, like a modern woman, is aware of sanitation and hygiene. She keeps her house in order and gives a towel bath to Panchi. The poor sanitary conditions of the village worry her. Gauri is, thus, a symbol of strength. She faces boldly all the hard blows of destiny and time with equanimity. She does not bow down before the brutalities either of her husband or of the society itself. She retains her individuality and dignity. Sinha calls her "an epitome of excellence, strength and virtue" (72). Again as "one of the most memorable female characters in the whole range of Indian Fiction" (Sinha, 70).

In sum, Gauri is the replica of a modern woman who refuses to be a fiddle and finally emerges as a bold, dignified human being. In the words of K.N. Sinha, *The Old Woman and the Cow* creates the legend of a heroic peasant woman in a small minded village. It has a definite epic strain to it. The closeness to Nekrasov's poem does not in any way diminish the richness and beauty of its original conception, based on the Sita myth which is woven like a central jewel into the whole design" (73). Gauri completed her journey from victimization to consciousness and broke from the dependence syndrome. Anand, thus, imparted voice to this voiceless creature to raise her voice against male chauvinism and go beyond the mythical belief of marriage as a domestic belief.

REFERENCES

Anand, Mulk Raj. *Gauri* (First published as *The Old Woman and the Cow* in 1960.) New Delhi: Arnold-Heinemann Publishers Pvt. Ltd., 1980. (All page references are from this edition.)

Lindsay, Jack. *The Elephant and the Lotus*. Bombay: Kutub-Popular, 1965.

Sinha, K.N. *Mulk Raj Anand*. Delhi: Kalyani Publishers Pvt. Ltd., 1995.

The Injured and Insulted: A Saga of Suffering in Anand's *Two Leaves and a Bud*

15

Neeraj Kumar

Mulk Raj Anand is an outstanding writer of Indo-Anglian fiction. He has been conscious of the need to help raise the untouchables, the peasants, the serfs, the coolies and other suppressed members of the society to the level of dignity and self-awareness in view of the abjectness, apathy and despair in which they are sunk. He worked for the cause of that section of society, which was injured, insulted and exploited. They suffered on grounds of age-old traditions and socio-economic barriers of caste, class, sex, and race. Deeply touched and moved by the situation of the suffering lot Anand condemned such social evils. As a true humanist he tried to create awareness among the people and also tried to find some amicable solutions to such problems. Instead of discarding them as outcaste Anand tried to integrate them with the mainstream of the society. To quote Iyengar:

> He wrote of the pariahs and the bottom dogs rather than of the elect and the sophisticated. He ventured into territory that had been largely ignored till then by Indian writers. For all their nationalistic fervour, Bankim Chandra's novels were but romances.... Tagore was chiefly interested in the upper and middle classes, Premchand chose his themes from the peasantry and humble folk of U.P. None of them cared to produce realistic or naturalistic fiction after the manner of a Balzac or Zola. (333)

Anand's masterpiece *Two Leaves and a Bud* has for its background the forests of Assam. It reveals the miserable plight of the labourers in the Tea plantations of Assam. Gangu, the hero of the story, crosses India horizontally from a village near Hoshiarpur in Punjab to the MacPherson Tea Estate in distant Assam. Whereas Bakha of *Untouchable* and Munoo of *Coolie* are mere boys, Gangu is past middle age. His wife Sajani and his children Leila and Buddhu also accompany him.

The novel opens with a philosophy—'Life is like a journey'. On the way to Assam he inquires lots of things from Buta, the Sardar of the MacPherson Tea Estate. It was he who had recruited Gangu and other coolies. Very soon, they all reach Garhi station. The Sardar leads all of them to small wooden shed where they meet Shashi Bhushan Bhattacharya, a mercurial being, with a thin body and a foxy face, with a wild shock of hair. He asks all of them to go to their billets, as they must be tired. The tea plantation is a world within a world that is more a prison as Narain, a coolie from Bikaner tells Gangu:

> I suppose it was in our kismet. But at home it was like a prison and here it is slightly worse. First water, afterwards mire! This prison has no bars, but it is nevertheless an unbreakable jail.... (Anand, 1998:38-39)

Very soon Gangu and other coolies adjusted themselves to the working of the Tea Estate. Sunday is a holiday so most of the coolies prefer to go to the bazaar in the village of Bedhi, two miles east of the tea estates. The children and especially the wives of the coolies are very happy. They get a chance to buy numerous things for the household. After coming back, due to the over strain, Gangu developed fever. His heart throbs and his temples ache like a heap of cracking wood enveloped in a leaping inextinguishable fire (80).

His wife pressed his legs, and his daughter massaged his head with oil. Soon the fever left Gangu and caught Sajani. She developed cholera and died. It was so sudden that Gangu was dumb with the shock. He was blinded and could not at first believe that she whom he had come to regard as immortal from the habit of nearness could have lapsed into an utter and ultimate silence and become *swargbashi*. For a time, he moved in a trance, beckoning the despair of bereavement to come and take possession of him. He had to do his wife's funeral; for this he went to the office for a loan of twenty rupees. There he was asked for a *najarana*. Since Gangu neither had cash nor any other security to give he was denied even a single pie. Rather he was driven away by Charles Croft Cooke, the Burra sahib,

> You bloody fool, get out! Get out! You have been spreading infection all over the place.... By whose orders did you come here? (114)

Even after getting humiliation at Croft Cooke's hands, he dared not think of wreaking vengeance on the sahib as he considered himself responsible for this. He went to Buta too, for a loan but he also refused. At last Gangu had to carry the dead body of his wife to the cremation ground. He felt choked in his throat with the memory of his wife and his eyes filled with tears.

Gangu was very much perturbed by his wife's sudden demise. 'Each one is happy or miserable in his own skin' (169), he muttered to himself. He had been weakened by life into an accepting character. For working under a torrid sun, sowing, reaping attending to a hundred different jobs, fighting nature had taught him patience and endurance, virtues which make for dour hearts but weak wills. He was worried about his two children especially his daughter Leila. To him she is Sajani's gift to him, to tend him in his old age (146).

Leila too had become lonely in the house after her mother's death. She had wept bitterly when Sajani died; she had cried for days as each little thing she did in the house which her mother had done before, reminded her of the fact that her mother was no more. She often sang

> Mother, O Mother
> O my mother
> Whenever the memory of you comes to me.
> There is a sudden pain in my heart.... (159)

She felt as if she could see the warm presence of Sajani close to her and who seemed to say, "Never mind, my beautiful, you will be happy, I have told your father to betroth you and you will soon be married and go to your husband's home. But mind you look after your old father and your little brother, now that I am no more" (161). One can find a new light in Leila's eyes.

The way she bruises the python symbolizes a revolutionary message.

Gangu often became nostalgic after his wife's death—recalling his bullocks and plough to till with, the small lichen growing on the edge of the wall, Bhola, the toothless village dog running across the fields in search of an imaginary rabbit and shy women threshing the hay in the sun. He also cursed Buta, who, to him, had wept like a hypocrite at the death of Sajani 'The liar', Gangu burst forth, 'he killed my Sajani with his lies'. He further added:

> She was unhappy from the very moment she arrived here, though she didn't say so, because she did not want to hurt me. And then she took my illness and died. (143)

Moreover, Gangu was a man of self-respect. One day when Narain narrated the atrocities of Sardar Buta who beat Suleman, a fellow coolie for no fault of his, Gangu was suddenly reminded of his own beating at the hands of the Manager Sahib. However, he did not want to think of that incident because the Rajput in him, who should have retaliated, had been prevented from doing so by the calamity of his wife's death. He knew it very well how the insult latent in the beating hurt a man more than the actual pain of the blow. The kicks had bruised his body, no doubt, but it was the humiliation of having always to lower his eyes before the man who had beaten him. To remain silent, to suffer and to stifle the bitterness of his experience to forgive—that was now his innermost instinct. Forgiveness to him was not fickleness. He often reminded the proverb, 'Men with abiding purpose cherish neither hatred nor love...they forgave lightly. But forgiveness did not mean that they should cease to strive against wrong. Indeed, true forgiveness was a hard battle...to be humble and not proud in forgiveness' (173).

In the Assam Valley Tea Garden, Reggie Hunt, the assistant planter was a dominating voice. The wives, sisters and mothers of the coolies were not safe in the valley. He was so cruel that once he gave order to the warders to strike them. He himself rode his horse into the thick of the crowd, trampling on the men, women and children who pushed and grovelled and ran in utter confusion. The sobbing, moaning mob of hurt and broken creatures seemed to waver helplessly before this image of Reggie's ferocity. All the coolies rushed towards the Manager's office. But there they got nothing except the beating with the barrel ends of the rifles. In the turmoil, one coolie had died and several others wounded. At the initiative of Gangu, they went to Dr. De La Havre. He, on hearing about the incident, felt a dismal wave of futility and the utter invisible ache of helplessness. He encouraged them to report the matter to the *Bara sahib* and also to abstain from working till justice is given to them. They all crawled away towards the Manager's office. But their power and courage—all disappeared the moment they saw Reggie Hunt and Croft Cooke. Some of them started retracing their steps, while the rest fell back, stumbling, shrieking, hysterical, craven and defeated. Narain very well remarked, "There was nothing to be done except to make up their minds to settle down there and smoke the *hookah* and mention the name of Ram" (213).

De La Havre, a man of positive nature, felt that they all had been brought up to be what they are by the sweat of these coolies. Once when Gangu came to him for some financial help to pay off his loan of twenty rupees, he immediately gave him ten rupees and eight annas. He also assured him to do some thing about a piece of land for him. He was very critical of the system. On account of his pronounced sympathy with the coolies, he was dismissed and his romance with Barbara came abruptly to an end. Though he tried his best to make her recall their relationship but of no use as she was not ready to give up all her relationships for the sake of his love.

Gangu in spite of his best efforts could not improve his lot. Life settled down once more to its ordinary routine of dullness for him. He had accepted everything else without even so much as a gesture of complaint. His condition was a constant source of anxiety to his daughter who thought he was going mad and to his son who believed that he had become possessed of a *ginn* or a *bhut*. Gangu, too, often mumbled:

> Who are you, who look towards me?... What have I done, oh! Can't you spare me? My heart is weeping. My wife is dead! My children are young. (247)

And suddenly he would get frightened and would begin to walk back as if the oncoming horded were going to rush at him. He would begin to count the beads of imaginary rosaries and would cry out:

> Lord, God, deliver me, save me from the wrath of my enemies.... (247)

He very often thought at the working of the Almighty. He said that though the earth was bought and sold and confiscated God never meant that to happen, for He did not like some persons to have a comfortable living and the others to suffer from dire poverty. He had created land enough to maintain all men and yet many die of hunger and most live under a heavy burden of poverty all their lives as if the earth were made for a few and not for all men.

Charles Croft Cooke had organized a hunt in the honour of His Excellency, Sir Geoffrey Boyd, and the Governor of Assam. The latter had decided to inspect the gardens, particularly the disaffected areas, i.e. 'the scene of the mutiny'. Croft Cooke was happy as the Governor's visit would not only enhance his prestige in Anglo-Indian circles but also convey the dual policy of the government to the people—the policy of firm rule as well as a paternal regard for the welfare of His Majesty's subjects. All the coolies who had been engaged to organize the hunt were given five rupees as *bakhshish*. Besides, those men who were marked as *budmashes* during the mutiny were pardoned and half their fines remitted. This was done to stimulate goodwill between the sahibs and the coolies. Though Gangu was not too grateful for these gracious gifts as he still had part of the fine to pay off and the debts he had incurred for his wife's funeral, he had begun to accept everything without any complaint. He felt he wanted no gold, no silver but only food and to exist. But in his heart of hearts he kept on saying, 'Money is everything in this world' as if the phrase were loaded with all the suffering he had endured. He further added:

> It is the crux of the world—Gold. Gold is the living soul of man, the colour of rajahs and gazelle-eyed courtesans, beautiful to the sight.... It is gold that conquers understanding and understanding that achieves gold, so that in this wonderful world gold and understanding are but conditions of each other.... (264)

Reggie Hunt, too, had to pay for his cruelty. A sort of coldness had come to prevail between him and the rest of the English community ever since the riot. He held his father and his stepmother responsible for his miserable life. Though for the time being, he thought to go home, get married and then come back and be thoroughly respectable. That would certainly rehabilitate his position. But that was a question of money. Unless he had sufficient money, he could not afford to keep a wife. For him life was a sport and he wanted to be happy at any cost. He needed only three things—a spot of polo, a woman, and a drink and would damn everything else. Once, in a mad accession of lust he approached Leila while she was leisurely plucking the tea leaves alone. Seeing him she ran away but he followed her to her house. There, mad with lust and maddened by frustration and fear, he shot blindly in front of him and killed Gangu. The strain of irony is obvious when Reggie Hunt is discharged.

Like his other novels, *Two Leaves and a Bud* also, Anand has depicted two sets of characters, representing two different approaches to life. On the one hand we have positive characters like De La Havre, Gangu, and Narain who stand for what is good in life while on the other there are characters like Reggie Hunt, Croft Cooke, Buta who stand for cruelty. Just as Munoo, a village boy in *Coolie* goes out in such of subsistence and security but is crushed by powerful exploitative forces operating everywhere and dies of consumption Gangu, too, moves out and is ultimately killed. But this does not signify the end of individual spark. Gangu's zeal and zest for life can be found in these lines: "He gripped the handle of his spade with an unwavering faith and dug his foot into the sod made by a furrow and sensed the warm freshness of the earth that would yield fruit" (146). In *Coolie*, Munoo also longs for life "...looking at Mohan frank-eyed and helpless, clinging to him as if the mere touch of his friend's body would give him life" (318). Iyengar has rightly observed:

> There is something of Forster's *A Passage to India* in this novel—the atmosphere of suspicion and strife, the racial intolerance and antagonism, the small talk in the Club, the reign of prejudice and unreason.... (346)

REFERENCES

Anand, Mulk Raj. *Coolie*. Delhi: Arnold Publishers, 1988.

Anand, Mulk Raj. *Two Leaves and a Bud*. New Delhi: Arnold Associates, 1988. (All quoted lines are taken from this edition.)

Iyengar, K.R.S. *Indian Writing in English*. New Delhi: Sterling Publication, 1985.

Social Amelioration in Mulk Raj Anand's *Untouchable*

16

Pinki Negi and Sumitra Kukreti

Mulk Raj Anand born exactly a century ago in Peshawar received his higher education from Lahore, London and Cambridge Universities. Despite spending his formative years in England he ultimately chose a small village in western India as his permanent home. The period spent in England naturally generated a heightened awareness towards the pathetic status of outcasts poor and downtrodden people in pre-independence Indian society. "I found myself writing my novels and stories about the poor with some ease because I had actually lived with them and experienced their miseries" (Cowasjee, 26). Through his novels Anand has tried to depict the same pain and trauma of these people, which he himself experienced while living amid them. In his hands fiction became a medium of social amelioration. He took a revolutionary step by choosing his protagonist from 'the poorest of the poor class'. To quote Abidi:

> Anand wanted to write about the underdogs of society and his selection of an untouchable boy as the hero of his novel is within the boundary of his literary decision. An untouchable belongs to the lowest dregs of humanity. The very choice of theme is a bold stroke of genius. To make a sweeper the hero of his novel was a revolutionary departure for an Indian writer of the Nineteen-thirties. (86)

E.M. Forster in the Preface of *Untouchable* says:

> *Untouchable* could only have been written by an Indian, and by an Indian who observed from the outside. No European, however sympathetic, could

> have created the character of Bakha, because he would not have known about his troubles. And no Untouchable could have written the book, because he would have been involved in indignation and self-pity. (vii)

The novel *Untouchable* is one such fine example which reflects the sufferings and trauma of a sweeper boy, Bakha, who cleans the dirt of upper class and upper caste people and because of his job (scavenging), he is rejected, neglected and humiliated as a human being by the class conscious Hindus. "They think we are mere dirt because we clean their dirt" (70). This novel depicts a single day life experience of Bakha, the chief protagonist, who because of his lower birth not only undergoes mental humiliation but also physical sufferings at the hands of orthodox Hindus. The novel *Untouchable* is not only the story of Bakha but it represents the miseries and humiliation of all "the dispossessed and emphasizes the pernicious effects of discrimination, deprivation and a kind of denaturalization of moral and other cherishable values of a civilised society" (Paul, 18). According to Prof. Naik, "the central theme of *Untouchable* is the age-old injustice perpetrated by traditional Hindu society upon a whole class of people within its fold." Anand has presented the real rigid conventional contemporary Indian society, the system where untouchables had no place, no respect and no sympathy. They were brutally treated by the upper caste Hindus and were not endowed with the right to articulate or express their anger. The novel *Untouchable* is a beautiful description of the tragic plight of outcastes. The poor economic condition was one of the causes of their negligence as a being. They had to beg breads, which were generally flung upon them, which they had to pick-up from the roads. Poverty was a curse on them, which compelled them to eat the left over from the plates of upper castes. They were not permitted to access water from brooks or wells by themselves. Even for natural objects of life they had to wait for hours and hours for upper caste Hindus to get their pitchers filled with water. They could not fetch water from wells or brooks as according to the age-old tradition their touch could defile water. They could not dig their own wells, as it was an expensive affair for them. In a nutshell, it was only their poor economic condition and menial job, which transformed them into a disgusting object in the eyes of upper caste Hindus.

The novel is a merciless attempt to expose the heightened hypocrisy of the representatives and guardians of the Indian society. Pt. Kalinath, a priest, is one of the religious figures in the novel who is a shameless 'religious imposter'. He is a selfish man who drew water from the well to relieve his constipated stomach. He in the guise of a religious man was a sexual beast who searched a pretty face in the crowd and ultimately poured water in Sohini's pitcher and asked her to clean the courtyard of his house in the temple. Sohini who was an outcaste by birth felt grateful to him but soon her illusion shattered when Pt. Kalinath tried to molest her and later to save his honour hypocritically started shouting 'polluted, polluted'. He put the whole blame on the girl, Sohini and behaved as if she was trying to seduce him. Abidi says in this regard "in *Untouchable* there is Pt. Kalinath who wants to molest Sohini and the sexual union with an untouchable will not pollute him but when she refuses to yield to him, he cries of pollution" (48). Does this sexual attempt of Kalinath not prove him a debauch, which keeps his religion and beliefs at stake and tries to ravish a lower caste girl whose physical contact could defile him according to the rotten tradition and convention? The upper caste Hindus could not tolerate the presence of untouchables in the temple and believed that their presence defile the sanctity of it. Then why Pt. Kalinath remained scot-free as he himself had called a lower caste girl to clean the courtyard of his house, which was in the temple? Why his guilt (attempt to ravish a lower caste girl) was ignored by other upper caste Hindus? Does Kalinath's act of ravishing Sohini at such a pious place not imply that he was also ravishing the chastity and sanctity of the temple as "the temple, a symbol of the spiritual emancipation of man, has been turned into a rendezvous to exploit the virtuous like Sohini? Religion is used for exploitation of the naive and the ignorant" (Bamezai 80). Does this not present the sheer hollowness of Hindu religion? Does this not present the beastly treatment of one man towards another? The novel actually explores the hollowness of the Hindu religion and its followers who were under the false impression that only they had the right to worship God whereas untouchables pollute the temple even if they were within the sixty-nine yards of it. "A temple can be polluted according to the Holy Books by a low-caste man coming within sixty-nine yards of it..." (Anand, 53). Lord Rama did not hesitate to eat fruits by the hands of Shabri, an untouchable woman then why the followers and worshippers of the same Lord could not bear their presence in temple and hesitate to take things from their hands. Bakha who was keen to see the idols of gods was severely rebuked by the worshippers. "We are ruined. We will need to have a sacrificial fire in order to purify ourselves and our shrine" (53). Bakha's only fault lay in his lower birth, which subjected him to cruelty and injustice of upper caste Hindus. The acute awareness of his lower birth restrained him to retaliate the worshippers and take revenge on Pt. Kalinath. The age-old rotten customs protected men like Pt. Kalinath and in this way encouraged social injustice and exploitation of the lower depth people. Like temples, schools were also forbidden to untouchables, as the parents of upper caste students did not want their children to be defiled by the touch of the underdogs. Even the teachers were fearful of being contaminated by their physical contact. A teacher is given a god's place in Indian society, if he himself discriminates between touchables and untouchables, takes untouchability as a contagious disease and deprives them of their fundamental rights then who will come forth as a pioneer and disperse the idea that not the untouchables but untouchability is a stigma on society. The 'die-hard Hindus' had a very disgraceful behaviour towards lower caste community. Even before picking money given by untouchables, upper caste Hindus used to sprinkle water on them. The things were not given in their hands but were thrown at them. Bakha bought jalebis and knew that he had been cheated by the confectioner, he did not dare to complain him but simply because this was something very usual for the upper caste people to cheat the downtrodden and particularly the scavengers.

> He caught the jalebis which the confectioner threw at him like a cricket ball, placed four nickel coins on the

> shoe board for the confectioner's assistant who stood ready to splash some water on them, and he walked away embarrassed, yet happy. (37)

Bakha underwent the same humiliation and embarrassment when he went to beg breads. The woman did not want to trouble herself and therefore she flung the bread at him while shouting loudly, "Vay Bakya, take this. Here's your bread coming down" (65). He collected the bread from the pavement, which was very disgusting and humiliating. These incidents reflect the mental sufferings of downtrodden man, Bakha. The novel *Untouchable* is the story not only of an individual but it represents the miseries and trauma of the whole community. Anand as a novelist has very deftly portrayed the worst conditions of the untouchables who were badly suppressed by the higher caste Hindus. They had to announce their arrival while passing through a crowd. The crowd harshly punished Bakha when he accidentally touched an upper caste man. "The touched man gave him an indignant, impatient look and signed to him, with a flourish of his hand, to wait" (41). He tolerated the humiliation in the market without uttering a single word. If he had been an educated man he would have been able to retaliate back. But his mum and tolerating attitude promoted the cancerous growth of untouchability and blind faith in orthodox conventional views. Bakha did not attempt to weed out the evils of casteism from the society, as he was not able to understand that being a human being he was also equal to other beings. This shows that Bakha is somewhere satisfied with his position in the society as says Bamezai:

> Bakha has no inclination to rise in the caste hierarchy. His wish is to lead a normal life, which is not restricted by social taboos of denial of right to temple entry, inter-dining and walking freely and drawing water from the common wells. He is not able to articulate these wishes except the desire to go to school, but his defiance is against these restrictions. (60)

Undoubtedly education generates awareness and awakening in man and strengthens him to struggle against oppressive world. "This value in education will make learning a powerful tool of social reconstruction" (105). Mulk Raj Anand is a champion in depicting the doomed lives of oppressed and downtrodden people who were not considered human beings but creatures, born to serve upper caste Hindus. As a novelist Anand has very beautifully portrayed the pathetic condition of the people of lower stratum and caste. His works present him more a social reformer who has a mission to give them an equal place, equal respect and equal rights in the society through his emotion and pity evoking works. He has criticized "the social injustice which widens the gulf between man and man" (78) but on the other hand he also suggests that "a change in men's attitude towards his fellowmen as the only road to salvation" (77). Premila Paul has also assessed that the corrupting influence of casteism will culminate in "segregation and subjugation of thousands of people into perpetual misery and eventual extinction" (31). After going through the novel *Untouchable* it seems that Mulk Raj Anand has tried to enlighten class conscious Hindus who are the victims of their sick psyche and old conventional views. He has highlighted the evils of the Indian society and heartily wants to eradicate such evils, the evils which separate one man from another. He believes that to redeem the society from the burden of caste and class it is necessary to eradicate the evil of inequality and untouchability and to accept them as human beings with the same blood in their veins. This is the only means to enable us to empathize with them and the only path that would lead our society to progress.

REFERENCES

Abidi, S.Z.H. and P.P. Mehta. *Mulk Raj Anand's Untouchable: A Critical Study*. Bareilly: Prakash Book Depot, 2003.

Anand, Mulk Raj. *Untouchable*. New Delhi: Penguin Books, 2001.

Bamezai, Gita. *Mulk Raj Anand: The Journalist*. New Delhi: Kanishka Publishers, 2000.

Cowasjee, Saros. *Mulk Raj Anand: A Profile*. Bombay: *The Illustrated Weekly of India*, May, 1969.

Paul, Premila. *The Novels of Mulk Raj Anand: A Thematic Study*. New Delhi: Sterling Publishers, 1983.

Naik, M.K. *Mulk Raj Anand*. New Delhi: Arnold Heinemann, 1973.

Mulk Raj Anand: The Plight of Untouchables

17

Jaya Srivastava

The sweeper is worse off than a slave, for the slave may change his master and duties and may even become free, but the sweeper is bound for ever, born into a state from which he cannot escape and where he is excluded from all intercourse and the consolations of his religion (Forster 6).

Mulk Raj Anand, one of the most highly regarded Indian novelists writing in English is no more. He was one of the members of the grand troika of founders who inaugurated the canons of Indian fiction in English, the other two being R.K. Narayan and Raja Rao almost his contemporary. A man with commitment, Anand was a life-long crusader for the cause of have-nots. His main concern had always been for the creatures in the lower depths of Indian society who were once men and women: the rejected, which had no ways to articulate their anguish against the oppressors. Anand's sense of ache at the heart of Indian humanity, his understanding compassion for the waifs, the disinherited, the lost, in a word *Daridra Narayan*, the one visible god head omnipresent in Indian subcontinent truly made him a prophet who translated the pains of helpless to the world.

Born as the son of coppersmith who had served as a soldier in the British army, this circumstance gave Anand an appreciation of the tragedy of the Indian Caste system and also the possibility of an honourable exit from its conventions. Mulk Raj Anand's prolific writing career spanned more than seventy-five years, a rare achievement for a writer. He was a vocal supporter of the Gandhian non-violence movement for national liberation from British colonial rule and his socialist sympathies took him considerably beyond the ambit of gradualist reform by the Mahatma. It is the belief of many that if he was not branded a 'Left Wing Writer' opposing the British Imperialists in India, he would have got the Noble Prize for Literature.

Anand's career was launched by a family tragedy instigated by the rigid caste system that continues to be the scourge of Indian society even today. He wrote a moving essay in response to the suicide of an aunt who had been ex-communicated by his family for sharing a meal with a Muslim. Anand gained and an international following early in his life. His novels *Coolie* and *Untouchable* (1935) set an entire generation of educated Indians thinking about India's social evils that were perpetuated, in the name of religion and tradition. These and other early novels and short stories brought into sharp focus the dehumanizing contradiction within colonized Indian society. Through his writings he revealed that in addition to the foreign colonialism of Britain, there existed layers of colonialism within Indian society. This internal colonialism stood in the way of India's transition to a modern civil society. While expressing the over arching divide between the British and a colonized India, he reveals on Indian Society creating its own layers of colonizers and colonized thereby rendering the fledgling Indian Nationalism an extremely problematic concept.

Mulk Raj Anand speaking about the real test of the novelist once said:

> It may be in the transformation of words into prophesy. Because, what is writer if he is not the fiery voice of the people, who through his own torments, urges and exaltations by realizing the pains, frustration and aspirations of others and by cultivating his incipient powers of expression, transmutes in art all feelings, all thought, all experience thus becoming the seer of a new vision in any given situation. (Dhawan, 14)

There is no question that Mulk Raj Anand has fashioned with *Untouchable*, a novel that articulates the abuses of an exploited class through sheer sympathy in the traditionalist manner of the realist novel. He is indeed the fiery voice of the people who form the untouchable caste. The critically acclaimed novel won Anand the reputation of being India's Charles Dickens. E.M. Forster writes in the introduction of the *Untouchable*: "Avoiding rhetoric and circumlocution (this book) has gone straight to the heart of its subject and purifies it."

It is a chilling expose of the life of a member of India's lowest and most abhorred caste, the story of simple day in the life of Bakha, a toilet cleaner, who accidentally meets a member of the higher caste. But if the goal of the writer as Anand himself had stated is to transform 'words into prophesy' then the reader's struggle for meaning in the closing scenes of the novel becomes problematic. While writing *Untouchable,* Anand has tried to address a specific question—how to alleviate the exploitation of the untouchable class in India? He then proceeds to address this question through the dramatization of Bakha, the novel's central character. The three prophecies or solution posited by the novel—the rhetoric of Christian Missionary, Mahatma Gandhi and the poet Iqbal Nath Sarshar fail to present a prescription for the freedom accessible to the untouchable community.

In order to understand the meaning of the last section of *Untouchable* let us deconstruct the construction of Bakha, the protagonist, since his own honest and direct gaze objectifies his society:

> His virtues lay in his close-knit—sinews and in his long breath sense. He was thinking of everything that he had heard though he could not understand it all. He was calm as he walked along, though the conflict in his soul was not over though he was torn between his enthusiasm for Gandhi and the difficulties in his own awkward naïve self. (Anand, 157)

Anand closes the final scene of his novel by appropriating the inner conflict of Bakha and juxtaposing 'enthusiasm' with 'Naivete'. There is a subtle irony in describing Bakha in this manner for on one hand it carries a strong sense of hope, of self-awareness of the individual within the greater scheme of Hindu Society. What Bakha has endured throughout his day's journey has had an enormous effect on the way he appropriates himself within his own culture. The novel ends on a positive note with Bakha going home and narrating his story in the hope that some sort of resolution, or some notion of understanding will occur.

Though Bakha is a young protagonist, he is far from being an innocent child. Yet he has been constructed with such a damning perception of innocence—an uneducated victim of his community's frustration that he does not fit into the confines of a traditional hero. This is because for him there is no solid gratification or inner resolution gained by the obstacles faced by him. Further as Forster points out in the novel's preface, the reader has every indication that the next day and the day after that; will be identical to the first, so then, his only heroism lies in his ability to survive the actual day's events. His survival does not rely so much on his inner strength as an individual, but rather on the action of the others that surround him—individuals of higher caste, for example characters like Charat Singh determine his survival depending on the degrees of pity he is willing to dispense at any particular moment.

Anand creates a character in search of his won identity within the very structure that has eliminated the possibility of him having one. Bakha clearly has trouble accepting the identity allotted to him at his birth. He has a desire to be like the Tommies he sees in the village. The narrator tells us that "the Tommies have treated him as a human being and he had learnt to think of himself as superior to his fellow outcaste" (9). He attempts to adopt the 'fashun' of the Tommies. He naïvely assumes that the mere adoption of the outward signs of a sahib will garner him respect. Bakha is desperately trying to escape the connotations, which the title of the novel asserts over his identity. Bakha's desire to imitate the Tommies is important because "(he) can preserve his identity only to the extent that he can be conscious of his superiority", opines C.D. Narsimhaiah (112). However, Bakha comes to the painful realization that "except for the English clothing there was nothing English in his life" (112). Therefore, the importance Anand places on Bakha's quest for identity leaves the reader questioning the viability of Bakha as the most appropriate figure to challenge the abuses of untouchability. Further Anand has taken a great risk both socially and professionally in writing about the untouchables as a minority that had been under represented in much of Indian English literature produced till then. It is clearly evident from Anand's novel that untouchables are both an oppressed and exploited class.

In portraying this exploited class as fairly and representatively as possible, Anand has an obligation of sorts. He has achieved the reader's sympathy for Bakha's exploitation via the horrendous abuses that he is subjected to as an oppressed minority. But in choosing to depict Bakha as a naïve, uneducated identity seeking protagonist, Anand has diminished the reader's ability or Bakha's to be seen as an initiator of change. This portrayal of Bakha is somewhat intentional. Anand admits to having run over his manuscript with Mahatma Gandhi and making the changes, he states, "I read the novel to Gandhiji and he suggested that I should cut down more than 100 pages, especially those pages in which Bakha seemed to be thinking and dreaming like a Bloomsbury intellectural" (Dhawan, 11). In depicting an untouchable in this way Anand is undermining the possibility of untouchable class in taking part in destroying their oppression because he constructs them as incapable of intellectually identifying systematic sources of their oppression. W.E.D. Dubois insists in his essay "Education", "if we ever compel the world's respect it will be by the virtue of our heads and not heels" ("Education", 121). Although "human genius and possibilities are not limited by color, race or blood, they can be curbed if there is no exposure to education" (Dubois, "Race", 189). Bakha even as a young boy aspired to go to school. But his father told him, "Schools were meant for the babus, not for the bhangis" (Anand, 42). The impact of his being an 'untouchable' hits him with great force and he realized that as a sweeper's son he would be polluting the place of learning.

Even though Bakha is unable to articulate the words of Gandhi which put him at an immediate disadvantage, he is rebellious. This rebellion is however internal and uttered with a silent voice. After the novels 'pivotal' touching scene in the village market Bakha reacts to the event with anger: "the strength, the power of his giant body glistened with desire for revenge in his eyes, while rage, indignation swept over his frame" (52). He is depicted as having a smouldering rage within his soul and then he resorts to self questioning "Why was I so humble? I could have struck him." Bakha has potential for rebellion, yet Anand chooses to silence this rebellion. He comes to self revelation. "I am an untouchable! An untouchable? What good is this recognition if there is no possibility of it being overcome?" (52).

Coming back to the basic question which the novel asks, how to eradicate the oppression of the untouchables? Anand addresses these question *vis-à-vis* three choices presented to the untouchable class-conversion to Christianity, the rhetoric of Gandhi and the flush system suggested by the poet. However, all three of these solutions prove inadequate because they remove the option for untouchable to take action against their own oppression. According to the novel, the only way to alleviate untouchability must come from the hands of either the oppressors or from something beyond the untouchable's control and understanding.

The first solution to Bakha's agony of self-abasement and total frustration is conversion. Colonel Hutchinson, the Salvationist, asks Bakha to turn Christian and so end his caste. But "Bakha's eyes are keen enough to see the dichotomy of the Missionary's existence that is he living a miserable life with his hot tempered wife. He comes to believe that the religion of his father is in no way inferior to Christianity" (Singh, 40). Thus, replacing one faith with another will not solve the problem of untouchability, but will only further complicate the matter.

Then there is the representation of Gandhi who articulates that untouchability is both a moral and religious issue, 'the greatest blot on Hinduism' (Anand, 146). The untouchable was really the harijan 'man of god' and it is 'Satanic' to assume anyone that in Hinduism is born polluted. Gandhi then proceeds to criticize the untouchable, by saying that they have to 'cultivate habits of cleanliness', they must get rid of their 'evil habits' such as drinking liquor, gambling and eating carrion. In essence he advocates emancipation by purification. But Bakha says to his father "they think we are mere dirt because we clean their dirt" (79). Anand though a staunch supporter of Gandhi has Bakha questioning the Mahatma's speech: "but now, the Mahatma is blaming us. That is not fair. He wanted to forget the last passage that he had heard" (143).

Anand then proceeds to offer the last solution, Anand takes an opportunity to express his own Marxist inclinations: "Well, we must destroy the inequalities of birth and unalterable vocations. We must recognize an inequality of rights, privileges and opportunities for every one" (155). He advocates that a change in profession will free the untouchable and the way to achieve thus through the implementation of a modern sanitary system—the flush. Then the sweeper can be free from the stigma of untouchability and assume the dignity of status that is their right as useful member of a classless and casteless society. This last choice is most favoured by Anand. Social rebellion is a viable option and the closest Anand comes to articulating a Marxist revolution in India is marked in the figure of the poet. But he has only skimmed the surface of its possibilities, introducing the concept in the very last page of the novel without giving the protagonist or the reader enough time to conceptualize its implications.

Thus, within a small space, to be exact only 157 pages and one Joycean textual day, Anand has presented a world where notions that are frequently regarded as immutable, are seen as mobile. The difficulties of alleviating the stigma of untouchability are far too complex for one man alone to tackle. Literature in isolation is not capable of changing society and even today 70 years after the book's first publication, untouchability and caste still exist today in India. Nevertheless Anand's text does serve as a catalyst for change. Bakha is a rebellious individual who has the ability to achieve his goal of freedom yet the stifling of this rebellious nature asserts the inability of the untouchables to free themselves, this is in effect the classical post colonial conundrum. The following lines from Matthew Arnold's 'Stanzas from the grand Chartreuse' brilliantly capture the dilemma of the untouchables.

> Wandering between two worlds, one dead,
> The other powerless to be born,
> With nowhere to rest my head,
> Like these, on earth I wait forlorn (85-90)

Bakha is nothing else but a wandering figure amongst the following flux of oppressions. He is clearly disenchanted by the confines that the class-system has imposed on him and attempts to appropriate himself amongst the ruling English class. This produces a state of double alienation. As a result, he is both rejected from his own culture and repelled by the other. Bakha, therefore, exists on the periphery of both worlds as Forster also suggests "on the surface of the earth if not in the depths of the sky, a change is at hand" (Forster, viii).

REFERENCES

Anand, Mulk Raj. *Untouchable.* London: Penguin, 1940.

Dhawan, R.K. Ed. *The Novels of Mulk Raj Anand.* New York: Prestige.

Dubois, W.E.B. "Education" in Moon, Henry, ed. *The Emerging Thought of W.E.B. Dubois.* New Delhi, 1972.

Forster, E.M., "The Preface" in Anand Mulk Raj's *Untouchable.* New Delhi: Orient Paperback, 1970.

Narasimhaiah, C.D. *The Swan and the Eagle.* Delhi: Motilal, 1987.

"Race Pride" in Moon, Henry, ed. *The Emerging Thought of W.E.B. Dubois.* New Delhi, 1972.

Analysis of Subaltern Psyche in Mulk Raj Anand's *Untouchable*

18

Lucky Gupta

From time immemorial the creative writers have been dealing with the problems of drowntrodden. The word subaltern means 'of inferior rank' is a term adapted by Antonio Gramsci to refer to those groups in society who are subject to the hegemony of the ruling class. The term has been adopted to post-colonial studies from the work of Subaltern studies groups. Among the invariant features of this study, is the notion of resistance to elite domination. The Subaltern voices the protest against established norms and traditions. Writers from Mulk Raj Anand to Arundhati Roy in Indian Writing in English presented the subaltern psyche in their writings.

As early as December 1974, Dr. P. Machwe, the then secretary of the Sahitya Akademi, New Delhi commented on the basis of the author's interview that Anand's early novels, *Untouchable* and *Coolie*, opened windows and doors to let fresh air into the mausoleum, the sentimental house, of Indian fiction. He described these works as being not only earthly and realistic, but also important and refreshing in their human concern.

Anand's novels show his profound concern for and deep understanding of the problems that exists in Indian society. By a psychological insight of the very nature of the man, his novels deal with the emotions, feelings and psyche of human character. As a first work of fiction, Indian or Western, to take an outcast Subaltern as its chief character, *Untouchable* was and has remained a revolutionary novel. In Commonwealth literature Anand's *Untouchable* is the best example that deals with a Subaltern psyche struggling with his passions and obsessions.

Bakha is one individual against many. He represents the society where the individual is most weak and the society is most strong. He passes more of his time among caste Hindus and belong to the minority. He is one of more than sixty million *harijans* as he passes half his time in the novel among crowds of caste Hindus so the odds against him are very large. As a hero of the novel Bakha is given pages after pages of introspection as he struggles towards the realization of Untouchability. The alternative passion of experience of Bakha's introspection firmly shapes the novel.

The significance of the novel *Untouchable* rests on the realization of the concept of untouchability in Bakha's mind and hence in the mind of the reader. We find sympathized with Bakha and subaltern group he represents on one hand and on the other the colonial situation of Bakha with the bound of his own culture. Anand's presentation of untouchable Bakha is prototypal. Many things that happen to Bakha in the novel still happen somewhere or other even today. In the Preface to the book E.M. Forster wrote,

> *Untouchable* could only have been written by an Indian and by an Indian who observed from the outside. No European however sympathetic, could have created a character of Bakha, because he would not have known enough about his troubles. And no untouchable could have written the book, because he would have been involved in indignation and self-pity.

E.M. Forster again comments:

> ...the book seems to me indescribably clean...it has gone straight to the heart of its subject and purified it.

The early pages of novel show how a subaltern like Bakha (a sweeper) living in hard conditions has some rare qualities like sincerity and efficiency, the urge for life and an urge to rise above his station:

> "But Bakha was the child of modern India. The clear-cut style of European dress has impressed his naïve mind. This stark simplicity had furrowed his old Indian consciousness and cut deep new lines where

> all considerations, which made India evolve skirty costumes, as fitted for human body, lay dormant. But Bakha looked at the Tommies, stared at with wonder and amazement.... So he tried to copy them in everything." (2)

Bakha's psyche portrayed by Anand is not a dream to be a caste Hindu but a white Sahib. In Bakha's scale of value the white Sahib was far superior to a caste Hindu, and so in his heart he desires that he would not be a caste Hindu but a white Sahib. His imagination sees himself at least:

> ...clad in a superior military uniform cleaning the commodes of sahibs in the British barracks. (69)

Here we can find a colonial situation of a subaltern as a young man of eighteen, who had been:

> ...caught by a glamour of "white man's" life. The Tommies had treated him as a human being and he has learned to think of himself as superior to his fellow-outcastes statement. Otherwise, the rest of the outcastes...were contained with their lot. (02)

The first incident Anand takes in the novel 'the incident of polluting in the bazar' in which we can read the recollections of Bakha. It was the custom at that time that a sweeper had to beat the drum hung around his waist and guard others of his presence. One day Bakha buys some *jalebies* and as he was going to eat them in a happy mood, a Lalaji, a man of upper class was touched by him. Lalaji calls him 'swine, dog, dirty dog, son of a bitch, offspring of a pig'. The other upper caste people also begin to shower upon him the abuse and humiliation. At that movement Anand pitiably and efficiently expresses the feeling of Bakha:

> The cruel crowd, all of them abused, abused, abused. Why are we always abused? The sanitary inspector that always abused my father. They always abuse us. Because we are sweepers. Because we touch dung. They hate dung. I hate too. That is why I come here. I was tired of working in latrines every day. That is why they don't touch us; the high castes. (43)

Anand tries to invite the attention of the readers towards the mental state of Bakha and tries to underline the irony and pity of the situation that a lovable boy, honest, noble and efficient had to suffer all kinds of insults and humiliations only because he is a Subaltern. The repetition of the word untouchable delineates the agitation in the heart of Bakha. He is not a dead log like his father but very much alive. He feels and reacts:

> But there was a smoldering rage in his soul. His feeling rise like spurts of smoke from a half smothered fire in fitful jerks when the recollection of abuse or review he suffered kindled a spark in the ashes of remorse inside him. (42)

In dealing with the subaltern psyche Anand contrasts the innate decency of Bakha with the hypocrisy of priest who claims Bakha's sister had defiled him when he himself fondled the young girl's breasts. At this moment the author's observation of Bakha's state of mind gives three notes towards subaltern group:

1. Obsession by the upper class.
2. Retaliation.
3. Helpless situation.

This obsession raised, resolves Bakha to take revenge being thwarted by futility. The novelist has observed him as tiger but tiger at bay. When at the temple, Sohini tells Bakha about her molestation by the priest, his first reaction is, "I will go and kill him." Next moment however,

> He felt the cells of his body lapse back chilled. His eyes caught sight of the magnificent sculpture over the doors extending rights up to the pinnacle. They seemed vast and fearful and oppressive. He was cowed back. The sense of fear came creeping into him. He felt as if the gods were staring at him. (55)

The novelist again narrates:

> A super specimen of humanity he seemed whenever he made the high resolve to say something, to go and do something, his fine form rising like a tiger at bay. And

> yet there was a futility written on his face. He could not overstep the barriers which the conventions of his superiors had built-up to protect their weakness against him. He could not invade the magic circle, which protects the priest from attack by anybody, especially by a low caste man. So in the highest moment of his strength, the slave in him arrested itself, and he lapsed back, wild with torture, biting his lips, ruminating his grievances. (56)

The same note occurs in hockey match incident where Bakha saved a small boy for being crushed in stampede and takes him to his home. The boy's mother instead of rewarding Bakha for his admirable job rebukes him and accuses him for being the root of the trouble. The novelist also contrasts the rigidity of Hindu beliefs when the humane relations which developed casually between the harijans and other, "lesser breeds without the law", such as the Havildar and other Muslims, and among the boys who play hockey together. The treatment of humiliation of Bakha arouses irony upon pity in the novel. Bakha is caught in vicious circle from which there is no escape. Anand observes the same attitude of betel leaf seller from whom Bakha buys cigarettes to fling the packet at the untouchable, "as a butcher might throw the bone to an insistent dog sniffing round the corner of the shop (34).

In the novel, while dealing with a subaltern, Anand shows a sure grasped of psychology of the both caste Hindus and the untouchable. In his dealing with the later, the caste Hindus are armed with the feeling of six thousand years of social and class superiority, a feeling which refuses to accept the fact that this subaltern untouchable is a human being rather it insists on treating him like a sub-human creature, to be ignored or bullied or exploited as the occupation demands. Bakha's father Lakha cannot even dream of harboring of any resentment for treatment he receives from the world. Young Bakha and his experience, and being far more sensitive, regents his lot but the servility of centuries, which is ingrained in him paralyses him even when he vaguely thinks of retaliation. Since Anand understands the psychology of both the untouchable and caste

Hindu, his picture of relationship between them is objective and balanced. In full contrast with the hypocritical priest Pandit Kalinath, stands Havildar Charat Singh who is so far above caste prejudices as to ask Bakha to go and fetch pieces of coal from the kitchen for the hubble-bubble, and who actually pours tea out of his own tumbler into the pan in Bakha's hand. Bakha feels: "for this man, I wouldn't mind being a sweeper all my life. I would do anything to him" (96). Further more in spite of so much torment in the life of Bakha this eventful day brings some compensation also. He receives a brand new hockey stick from Charat Singh, his friend Ram Charan and Chota both who stand higher than him in social hierarchy, sympathized with him and consoled him.

In the end there is a glamour of new hope in the three solution proposed. Like Ulysses the novel dealing with the events of just one day begins with the note of despair and ends with the hope of echoes of Shelley's West Wind. The problem of cast poverty, backwardness, ignorance, superstition admits of no easy solution. Almost 70 years after Anand's novel written in 1935 the problem with blunted edges still requires a firm and final solution. In the last, Bakha becomes aware of possible modern approaches to his problem, the town indicating the aspect of modernity. An intelligent and sensitive Bakha hates his lot. The particular day brings him additional torments yet in the end it also suggests solutions to his problems. The following suggestions came in hand:

1. Bakha to turn a Christian and so end his caste.
2. There is Mahatma Gandhi who is addressing a public meeting, which Bakha attends, says, "I regard untouchability as a greatest blot on Hinduism" (137). If he is to be born again, he would prefer to be born as outcaste. Hearing this, "Bakha was thrilled to the very marrow of his bones. That the Mahatma should want to be born as an outcaste" (138). It was satanic to think that anybody was polluted or could pollute another.
3. The third solution by poet Iqbal Nath Sarshar that, when scavenger changes their profession, they will end

> their caste and a modern sanitary system, the flush, will bring about this solution. "Then the sweepers can be free." The poet concludes, "from the stigma of untouchability and assume the dignity of status that is their right as useful members of a casteless and classless society". (146)

The spiritual message given by Gandhi makes Bakha in the last chapter accept his lot with the hope of escaping from latrines when they are converted to flush system. Bakha is duly impressed, feels more hopeful of the future than at any time since the day down, and returns to his house to tell his father about the Mahatma and about the machine that will "Clear dung without anyone having to handle it." Defending this epilogue in his Foreword to the book, E.M. Forster rightly says:

> It is a necessary climax, and it has mounted up with triple effect. Bakha returns to his father and his wretched bed, thinking now of the Mahatma, now of the machine. His Indian day is over and the next day will be like it, but on the surface of the earth if not in the depths in the sky, a change is at hand.

The more important thing in the last is the calmness that descents on Bakha at the end of the day of crises. It also makes him abandon his hope of becoming a "gentleman" of wearing the cloths of the sahibs and imitating them. Bakha discovers his self-identity from an original psychic state of ignorance and fights against a hostile social environment to discover a world of new freedoms. *Untouchable* thus can be observed as a memorable incident of one day that represents the subalterness of Bakha's individuality expressing the concept of untouchability.

REFERENCES

Anand, Mulk Raj. *Untouchable*. New Delhi: Penguin Books India, 2001. (All the subsequent references from the text are cited from this edition.)

Interview with Dr. P. Machwe at his office in the Sahitya Akademi, New Delhi.

Marriage as a Perennial Paradise: A Myth—A Study of Mulk Raj Anand's *Gauri*

19

Anuradha Verma

Numerous writers of the twentieth century started exposing the social evil in their writings. They dramatized the plight of the deprived classes and indicated the society for heaping indignities upon the oppressed. These portraits enable us to see the oppressed, the downtrodden and subalterans as humans not just helpless victims but men and women with their specific individuality. Mulk Raj Anand, Shivram Karanath, T. Shiv Shankar Pillai and others wrote moving accounts of the ugliness, squalor and the misery of their lives. *Untouchable, Coolie, Two Leaves and a Bud*, etc. are his novels which deal with the oppressed and underprivileged class.

Mulk Raj Anand, the crusadar of the downtrodden and a great Marxist and humanist is one of the three great Indian writers (Raja Rao and Narayan) of fiction writing in English. He is India's most controversial novelist. Bakha, Gangu, Munoo are the memorable character delineated by Anand. Mulk Raj Anand, the creator of memorable male character, portrays for the first time a woman in all her tenderness and resilience.

Gauri in the author's own words is:

> "My offering to the beauty, dignity and devotion of Indian women."

The story of the docile Gauri is a new kind of legend, wrung out of tragedy in a small village. The girl pits herself against the patriarchal Ramayana legend in which, the heroine is ultimately banished because she has lived in another man's house for some time. The gentle Gauri walks out and chooses to live on her own and to depend on herself.

The Old Woman and the Cow (*Gauri*) creates the legend of a heroic peasant woman in a small minded village. It has a definite epic strain to it. The closeness to Nekrasov's poem *The Peasant Woman* does not in any way diminish the richness and beauty of its original conception based on the Sita myth which is woven like a central jewel into the whole design.

Marriage in India is considered a very sacred institution. A woman should be *Pativrata*. A woman (wife), if adjusts according to man and bears all his (husband's) idiosyncrasies, accusations, becomes an ideal wife. The conservative society though stepped in twenty-first century still believes "*Pati* as *Parmeshwar*". The truth is that in majority of the cases the success rate of marriage depends on a woman.

In India the devotion of a wife to marriage institution is remarkable. Indian woman is not only a master of household but also manages outdoor jobs efficiently. It is generally seen that a house is never shattered if there is a woman to look after it. She can like a man work and earn as well as look after her some. But a husband cannot take care of home and in the absence of wife, his home is shattered. Indian marriages are considered to be made in heaven. It is one of the 16 sacraments (Sanskar) in Hindu religion. Marital life is one of the four Ashrams. But it is a myth to consider marriage as a perennial paradise.

This article gives a deep insight into the marital relations (life) of Panchi-Gauri. Was marriage a paradise or hell for her is studied here? The role of Gauri (as a wife) and Panchi (as a husband) in their marriage (marital life) is projected in this paper.

Gauri, gentle and good like a cow, is given away in marriage to Panchi, a temperamental youth of the village of Chota Piplan in the foothills of Himalayas. She puts up with everything at her husband's home and settles down patiently to a life of unremitting toil, hunger and pain. The situation, however, worsens because of drought and famine. Gauri's meekness makes her vulnerable to abuses and beatings at the hands of her husband. Even her chastity is doubted. She pleads innocence in vain. She is sent back to her mother's home in the village of Piplan Kalan. A worse fate awaits her there as her mother, under the evil influence of her uncle, Amru, sells her to "a respectable old man" who takes her to Hoshiarpur. Unable to win her love by courtship, the old lecher tries to outrage her modesty; she finally resists and angrily leaves the house. She finds shelter in the clinic of Colonel Mahindra and is employed as a nurse. Her beauty provokes Dr. Batra, the Colonel's Assistant, who attempts to rape her. Her own resilience, however, saves her from the nearly impossible situation. Later, she is restored to her husband through the agency of her now penitent mother. Colonel Mahindra, for whom Gauri has the highest respect and admiration, gives her a helping hand, but the union with her husbands proves to be a temporary affair. Panchi's ambivalence torments him still. Prompted by the village gossip, he demands proofs from her chastity again. Gauri would prove her chastity if she could, but the mother earth would not open her womb for her as she had done for Sita. In the moment of crucial decision, Gauri walks out of Panchi's life, though she is bearing his child in her womb. She returns to Colonel Mahindra's clinic and resumes her job as a nurse.

Gauri was truly a bovine. She thought that like Meera, she could win Panchi by her devotions. But her submissiveness could not win Panchi. Kesaro, Panchi's aunt (Chachi) envied Gauri. She cursed Gauri for being inauspicious and causing harm to the family. She (Kesaro) even blamed her for the famine and drought. 'Gauri' evinces the mother-in-law and daughter-in-law syndrome. She complains Panchi and remarks vehemently:

> Control her, if you can!...This bride of yours.... She has begun to answer me now.... I would not have worried but today look at what she has done, this girl.

In India this mother-in-law and daughter-in-law syndrome is very much prevalent. Mothers pamper their sons even when they are grown-ups (adolescents) and want them to be mother's boy. Therefore, when the wife comes and the attention of the son is diverted, mother dislikes the new member (wife of the son) after his marriage. Kesaro, reminds us of *Sons and Lovers* where Paul's mother was also very much inclined towards him. The over concern for Panchi made Kesaro start up her hate campaign towards Gauri. Panchi also admits:

> And before Nikka was born, while my uncle was away in the army, she used to dote upon me and considered me as her son.... Perhaps, she is jealous now that another woman has come to the house.

She tells her own son Nikka:

> That sister-in-law of yours is a sweeper woman and unclean.

Panchi loved Gauri but at Kesaro's insinuations he kicked and battered her. At times even felt guilty but could never satisfy his guilt and so merely felt angry. He consoled her after severe beatings. The spark against injustice was within Gauri. She once exclaimed grudgingly:

> How long can I go on being patient against the nagging of that woman and your shoe beatings on her behalf?

Gauri uttered in a clear speech:

> Why did she have to marry you off to me, if she, if she wants two husbands.

Panchi favoured her after his abuses, vent-ups and beatings. He was like Manu (Manoher) in *The Dark Holds No Terrors* who loved Saru during the day time and sexually exploited in the bed. This sadist approach of Manu is like Panchi's who despite feeling guilty never reconciled.

Gauri bears Panchi's whims and idiosyncrasies. She even didn't bother to give Panchi, the only token of her marriage dowry. She happily sacrificed her gold ear-rings and gave to him thinking it would help him in the hard times. But after selling these ear-rings, some of the money was used in boozing and revelling. Both Rafique chacha and Panchi purchased wine out of that money. They were not punished for this ill act but on the contrary Panchi taunts Gauri as "betrayer of my salt" and was kicked on the back.

It was Panchi who commented after his beating to Gauri that:

> It is the duty of a husband to check his wife when she is wrong.

But this is not applied *vice versa*. An Indian wife is ideal only if she bears husband and never cross examines him.

It was always Gauri who compromised and endured and behaved like a true *Pativrata*. She believed in the worship of her husband. Panchi not only abused her but also broke the limits of doubts. Kesaro's continuous blames plunged him into the whirlpool of doubts. One day with a sudden uprush of cowardice, he thrust her away from him when Gauri came to press his legs and kicking her viciously said:

> Go to your mother's home, you of the evil stars! If the rains come then I shall not believe my aunt Kesaro.... If not I shall have died! And you and your brat can find on yourselves.

Was Gauri a commodity who when needed could be used otherwise thrown away? The respect for Panchi in Gauri's mind even after her turning out of home remains same. She never called him by his name. Paro mocked at her:

> A cow to be sure...
> He is to beat you up everyday and then send you home.

The rate of success of marriage in India is much higher than Western countries. If surveyed the credit of the success rate goes to Indian women. Indian woman like Gauri bears the vent-ups and oddities of her husband till her patience is given up. Indian woman like Gauri is submissive and docile. Gauri despite Panchi's accusations and thrashings loved him and desired to go to him when asked by Colonel Mahindra.

After returning from Hoshiarpur, once again Panchi behaved the same way as done earlier. His suspicious nature once again entangled him in the sea of doubts. He under the influence of wagging tongues of village gossips and the provoking statements of Rakhi, the mid-wife, Kesaro and Rajguru, begins to suspect her fidelity. He called her a bitch, thrashed and kicked her. He angrily outbursted:

> You have cut my nose, bitch from Piplan Kalan! What curse upon my fate prospered in my marriage with you! Daughter of a whore!

This time Gauri stood up like a modern woman of terrible strength. She became defiant and left the place which could not give her due respect. Gauri is the incarnation of Sita, as it were, in an infirm, evil, and degenerate world. Jack Lindsay comments:

> Here the key-pattern lies in the tale from the Ramayana of the wife who is banished because she had innocently lived in another man's house. The blind circle is ended. The woman who is banished becomes the woman who herself rejects the narrow world.

Gauri is the modern vision of Sita not the self-effacing Goddess of *The Ramayana*. The earth swallows her up, indicating her honour. But this does not happen in the case of Gauri, however much she might will it! She prefers to break the labyrinth of an eccentric design rather than live in perpetual shame in her husband's house who wantonly mistrusts her. It is truly a pilgrimage of hope and faith that she undertakes. She set on example for others to follow. The inner transformation of Gauri is achieved with grace and courage. She is undoubtedly one of the most memorable female characters in the whole range of Indian fiction.

At the moment of crisis she is firm and erosionless like a rock. She pushed off Seth and warned him:

> I am guided by the Goddess! So do not come near me. Or you will burn.

Gauri, like a modern new woman dared to tell her husband:

> If you strike me again, I will hit you back.

She tells him the last word before she quits:

> There is nothing to tell him. He turned me out and I have come back to him as pure as I went away.

She left little Piplan with a grieving heart and with tears in her eyes like Sita. Sita said Hoor Banu of Panchi:

> He is not foolish. He is weak, spoilt creature! He pretended to be a lion among the men of the village! I

> am not Sita that the earth will open up and swallow me. I shall just go out and be forgotten of him.

Thus, Gauri finally rises against the existing traditions and begins to lead an independent life.

Gauri was like Rukmani of *Nectar in a Sieve* and Jhanak of *Shadow from Ladakh* who protests against her husband's words and fights tooth and nail to save her honour. Anand's heroine shows more courage than R.K. Narayana's heroine, who under similar circumstances, can only sulk in the dark room and can do nothing bolder. Gauri's sufferings remind us of Gissing's *Thyrza* and Hardy's *Tess* as they have to suffer immensely for no fault of their own.

If Gauri is modern vision of Sita, Panchi is Rama lost. His love for Gauri is tainted with a tender voluptuousness and remorse from the very beginning. For Panchi marriage is just to seek physical pleasures while for Gauri it is based on equanimity. There is a difference between their mental levels as Gauri like Astha has now emerged and grown as a broad-minded rational person. Panchi, however, fights his own divided self. He is torn between love and strife, his loyalty to Gauri matched against his allegiance to the villagers. Panchi no doubt loved Gauri. There are several instances shown in the novel to justify it as his turning out of Rakhi, the mid-wife, picking mangoes for Gauri, his caressing and consoling after his beatings. When she is restored to him after a long absence, he expresses the true voice of his feeling:

> I have known darkness. Now you have come and set me on fire again.

His utterance gets even more passionate as he burns in desire for her:

> I fretted and fretted.... I beat my head against a wall one day in despair.... Now I can breathe. Come, come to me Gauri...I want you.

But the passion did not last, and the other side of his nature, tormenting, asserts itself, throwing away the felicity for ever. He is neither constant nor wise and like a base Indian, throws his pearl away. In sum, he is a foolish passionate young man who is more real than Gauri wrong-headed and faithless, but very human, hence real.

It is not the fault of Panchi alone in the collapsing of this marriage. It is the entire society who at times behaves so crudely to women as if they are no human beings. If Gauri is questioned about chastity why isn't Panchi? As it is male-dominated society men are free to ejaculate with damn anyone yet they are chaste. If Gauri like Sita is questioned on the basis of staying at another place and away from husband then even Shri Rama and Panchi were away from their wives. It is very apologizing to say that males are given the freedom to do everything.

Morals, ideals, restrictions are attached only to woman not man. Gauri could have stayed further with Panchi if she kept quiet and endured his beatings and accusations. But finally she grew, her reasons opened and her self-respect aroused that denied her to bear the foolishness of Panchi. She boldly like Saru of *The Dark Holds No Terrors* left Panchi's home in order to be free from her husband's whims. Paro truly defined a woman's plight by saying.

> Suffering for us, sister, suffering, only suffering for us women.

Long back since the dawn of civilization, man realised the physical impotency of woman and has tried to rule her on its basis. Though today woman empowerment and emancipation are talked of yet we find so many rape cases, female infanticide, wife batterings, eve teasings, female harassment and suppression everywhere. Woman is not an inferior being but a human being with a different body structure. Nature has made her so tender in order to run the life process. It is a woman who reproduces and gives birth to children and runs a family lineage. This attribute of a woman should not be focused so to call her a weak physical being. A woman is also a human to have ego, self-respect and emotions. She is superior and potential if ignored this physical aspect. The endurance and perseverance to make her home, her marriage a paradise is remarkable.

Indian marriages are considered very sacred institution. This bliss is till the wife remains subordinate to her husband.

Today marriage means participating in all activities together, understanding, caring and sharing of two opposite sex. None is superior in it. Marriage can become a paradise if the two wheels (husband and wife) walk together with love, compatability and understanding on the road of life. It can also be a curse if anyone of the two goes out of track. Today women are not subjected to compressions and subjugations but like Nora has the desire to say:

> Let us sit down and discuss.

Thus, the marriage of Gauri-Panchi was not a paradise but a failure. It collapses when the bovine Gauri becomes Nora.

REFERENCES

Anand, Mulk Raj. *Gauri.* Bombay: Kutub Publishers, 1970.

Bande, Usha. *Giving Voice to the Voiceless*—A Review.

Sinha, K.N., *Mulk Raj Anand.* New Delhi: Kalyani Publishers, 1995.

List of Contributors

Mohammad Rizwan Khan Ph.D, is a Reader in Department of English, Aligarh Muslim University, Aligarh. He has been teaching for nineteen years. He has authored two books: *Policy and Provision for ESL in India's Higher Education* and *Study Skills*. He has taught at Nizwa in Oman and at Abha in KSA. He edits a biannual journal *Readings* published from Aligarh. He has worked on a project of Hornby Trust, London. He has published and presented many papers in various national and international forums on ELT, Drama, Indian Poetics, Indian Writing in English and Diaspora.

Saros Cowasjee, Professor Emeritus of English, University of Regina. He was a Visiting Commonwealth Professor in University of Aarhus, Denmark in 1975. He was awarded J.N. Tata Scholarship for postgraduate studies at Leeds University. He has been the recipient of four Canadian Council Leave Fellowships. He is one of the most prominent critics on Anand as he was appreciated by Anand himself. He has authored many books and anthologies on Anand and various other writers.

Dolly Sahair, was Mulk Raj Anand's life-long associate and confidante who worked on *Marg* for a long time with him. Dolly died of heart attack on a flight in May, while on her way to be with Mulk after a short visit to the U.S. Mulk died four months later.

Shiv K. Kumar, Renowned poet and novelist. He has immense contribution to Indian English Writing. He has also authored several books on criticism and translation studies.

A.S. Dasan, Teaches in the University of Mysore. Currently, he holds the honorary chairmanship of **Lokayata,** founded by Mulk Raj Anand. He is author of the book, *The Rains and the Roots*—The Indian English Novel *Then and Now* (2006), co-editor of the book, *India—A People Betrayed* (1993), author of a book, *Mulk Raj Anand—Profile of a Dissenting Pilgrim-Artist*, and co-editor (along with Prof. Amrik Singh) of another book, *Rereading Mulk Raj Anand—Recent Critical Considerations.*

Meenakshi Mukherji, Literary critic now based in Hyderabad. She was a Professor of English, Jawaharlal Nehru University, Delhi. Among her books are *The Twice-born Fiction, Realism and Reality*, *The Perishable Empire* and *Rereading Jane Austen*. Her book, *Elusive Terrain: Culture and Literary Memory* was published by Oxford University Press in 2007.

G.S. Balram Gupta, Retired as a Professor in English, from Gulbarga University, Karnataka. Presently he is the Editor of the *Journal of Indian Writing in English* and the Director of National Institute of Indian English Literature. He has authored/edited around a dozen books in the area of Indian English Literature.

Tutun Mukherjee, Professor and Head, Centre for Comparative Literature, University of Hyderabad, India. Her specialization in Literary Criticism and Theory urged her research interests in Translation, Women's Writing, Theatre and Film Studies, which have very often become contiguous subjects for her to teach and discuss.

Jasbir Jain, Writer and critic, has worked extensively on feminist, postcolonial, dramatic studies and on Indian literatures in Indian languages. Her recent publications include *Beyond Postcolonialism: Dreams and Realities of a Nation* (2006), *Reading Partition/Living Partition* (2006) and *Gendered Realities, Human Spaces: The Novels of Shashi Deshpande* (2004). Currently she is working on *Roots of Feminism.*

R.C.P. Yadav, Retired as the Head of the Department of English. He has authored a book on Mulk Raj Anand entitled *The Body-Soul Drama* and has extensively written on Anand's works.

Binod Mishra, Assistant Professor in English at IIT, Roorkee. He has been teaching English at various levels for the last twelve years. His Ph.D is on Pattern of Despair and Delight in the novels of Mulk Raj Anand which has come out as a book also. He has also to his credit many books and anthologies. He is also the editor of *Musings: An Anthology of Poems.*

Raihan Raza, Reader in Department of English, Aligarh Muslim University, has been teaching for twenty five years. Her special area of interest is modern poetry. She is working on Sylvia Plath. She also has interest in the Indian Writing in English. She has published various papers on Sylvia Plath, Mulk Raj Anand, W.H. Auden, post colonialism and dyslexia.

Rahmat Jahan, he has been teaching English under Magadh University service for more than seventeen years and is posted at G.B.M. College, Gaya (Bihar). She has authored three books. Besides, she has published various critical papers in journals of national repute and has presented papers in national and international seminars and conferences.

Jaya Srivastava, Reader and Head, English Department, Mahila Vidyalaya Post Graduate College, Lucknow. She has been teaching since 1977. She has publications in Indian Writing in English and American literature.

Syed Afroz Ashrafi, Lecturer in English at Commerce College, Magadh University, Patna. He is a poet and short story writer himself, and has also come up with a couple of his compilations and has also authored some anthologies of critical essays.

Sumitra Kukreti, Reader and Head, Department of Applied English in MJP Rohelkhand University, Bareilly. She has been teaching for seventeen years. She has authored two books and many research papers in national and international journals. She is actively engaged in supervising doctoral researches.

Lucky Gupta, Senior Reader in the Department of English, Shri Tikaram PG College (Dr. Bhimrao Ambedkar University), Aligarh. She has Ph.D on Emily Dickinson's Religious Vision and has been teaching for eighteen years. She has presented several papers at national/international seminars and conferences. She has a book to her credit and has contributed articles to journals.

Malti Agarwal, Reader and Head, Department of English, N.A.S. (P.G.) College, Meerut. She has been teaching English Literature for thirty three years. She has authored several books,

Anuradha Verma, Lecturer in N.A.S. (P.G.) College, Meerut, Uttar Pradesh. She has seven years of experience in teaching. She has participated in several seminars with presentations and has got papers published.

Pinki Negi, Lecturer in English in Bareilly, Uttar Pradesh.

Neeraj Kumar, Lecturer in the Department of English, Magadh University, Bodh Gaya, Bihar

G.L. Goutam, Senior Reader in Lajpat Rai P.G. College, Sahibabad, Uttar Pradesh.

